The Spanish Prisoner

American Indies

Series Editors: Gary Needham and Yannis Tzioumakis

Titles in the series include:

The Spanish Prisoner
Yannis Tzioumakis

978 0 7486 3368 5 (hbk)
978 0 7486 3369 2 (pbk)

Brokeback Mountain
Gary Needham
978 0 7486 3382 1 (hbk)
978 0 7486 3383 8 (pbk)

Forthcoming titles include:

Lost in Translation
Geoff King
978 0 7486 3745 4 (hbk)
978 0 7486 3746 1 (pbk)

Far From Heaven
Glyn Davis
978 0 7486 3778 2 (hbk)
978 0 7486 3779 9 (pbk)

Memento
Claire Molloy
978 0 7486 3771 3 (hbk)
978 0 7486 3772 0 (pbk)

The Spanish Prisoner

Yannis Tzioumakis

Edinburgh University Press

© Yannis Tzioumakis, 2009

Edinburgh University Press Ltd
22 George Square, Edinburgh

www.euppublishing.com

Typeset in 11/13pt Monotype Baskerville by
Servis Filmsetting Ltd, Stockport, Cheshire, and
printed and bound in Great Britain by
the MPG Books Group

A CIP record for this book is available from the British Library

ISBN 978 0 7486 3368 5 (hardback)
ISBN 978 0 7486 3369 2 (paperback)

The right of Yannis Tzioumakis
to be identified as author of this work
has been asserted in accordance with
the Copyright, Designs and Patents Act 1988.

Contents

Series Preface

In recent years American independent cinema has not only become the focus of significant scholarly attention but as a category of film it has shifted from a marginal to a central position within American cinema – a shift that can be also detected in the emergence of the label 'indie' cinema as opposed to independent cinema. The popularisation of this 'indie' brand of filmmaking began in the 1990s with the commercial success of the Sundance Film Festival and of specialty distributor Miramax Films, as well as the introduction of DVD, which made independent films more readily available as well as profitable for the first time. At the same time, film studies started developing courses that distinguished American independent cinema from mainstream Hollywood, treating it as a separate object of study and a distinct discursive category.

Despite the surge in interest in independent cinema, a surge that involved the publication of at least twenty books and edited collections alongside a much larger number of articles on various aspects of independent cinema, especially about the post-1980 era, the field – as it has developed – still remains greatly under-researched in relation to the changes of the past twenty years that define the shift from independent to 'indie' cinema. This is partly because a multifaceted phenomenon such as American independent cinema, the history of which is as long and complex as the history of mainstream Hollywood, has yet to be adequately and satisfactorily documented. In this respect, academic film criticism is still in great need to account for the plethora of shapes, forms and guises that American independent cinema has manifested itself in. This is certainly not an easy task given that independent film has, indeed, taken a wide variety of forms at different historical trajectories and has been influenced by a hugely diverse range of factors.

It is with this problem in mind that 'American Indies' was conceived by its editors. While the history of American independent cinema is still being written, with more studies already set to be published in the forth-coming years, and while journal articles are enhancing our understanding of more focused aspects of independent filmmaking, the American Indies series has been created to provide the necessary space to explore and engage with specific examples of American 'indie' films in great depth. Through this format, American Indies aims to encourage an examination of both the 'indie' text and its contexts, of understanding how 'indie' films operate within a particular filmmaking practice but also how 'indies' have been shaping a new formation of American cinema. In this respect, American Indies encourages a detailed examination of industrial, economic and institutional concerns alongside the more usual formal and aesthetic considerations that have historically characterised critical approaches of independent films. American Indies is a series of comprehensive studies of carefully selected examples of recent films that reveal in great detail the many sides of the phenomenon of the recently emerged American 'indie' cinema.

As the first book series to explore and define this aspect of American cinema, American Indies has had the extremely difficult task of producing a comprehensive set of criteria that informs its selection of titles. Given the vastness of the field, we have made several editorial decisions in order to produce a coherent definition of this new phase of American independent cinema. The first such choice was to concentrate on recent examples of independent cinema. Although the word 'recent' has often been used to include films made in the post-1980 period, as editors we decided that the cut-off point for films to be included in this series would be the year 1996. This was an extremely significant year in the independent film sector, 'the year of the independents,' as was triumphantly proclaimed by the *Los Angeles Business Journal* in February 1997, for a number of reasons. Arguably, the most significant of these was the entrance into the film market of Fox Searchlight, a new type of specialty film division created by 20th Century Fox in 1994 with the explicit intention of claiming a piece of the increasingly large independent film market pie. After a shaky start, Fox Searchlight would eventually achieve this objective through the production and distribution of films that followed many of the conventions of independent film as those were established after the success of *sex, lies and videotape* in 1989. These conventions had since then started being popularised by a number of films produced and distributed by Miramax Films, an independent company that was taken over by Disney after the phenomenal box-office success of several of its films at approximately the same time as 20th Century Fox was establishing its specialty division.

The now direct involvement of entertainment conglomerates like Disney and Fox in the independent film sector had far-reaching effects. Arguably, the most important of these was that the label 'independent', which for critics and the cinema-going public (wrongly) signified economic independence from major film companies like Disney, Fox, Paramount, Universal, etc., obviously ceased to convey this meaning. Instead, critics and public alike increasingly started using the label 'indie', which suggested a particular type of film that adhered to a set of conventions, as well as a transformed independent cinema sector that was now driven by specialty companies, most of them subsidiaries of major entertainment conglomerates. It is this form of 'independent' cinema, which has produced some of the most interesting films to come out of American cinema in recent years, that American Indies has set out to explore in great depth and that explains our selection of the label 'indies' instead of 'independents'.

We hope readers will enjoy the series

Gary Needham and Yannis Tzioumakis
American Indies Series Editors

Acknowledgements

In my capacity as the series co-editor and co-creator, I offer my deepest thanks to Gary Needham, a great scholar, colleague and friend, for coming up with the idea for American Indies and for inviting me to participate in his vision. I am extremely grateful to Edinburgh University Press for commissioning the series, as well as a number of other books in the field of American independent cinema.

A number of film and media scholars have contributed in various ways to this project. Gary Needham consistently provided constructive comments on various chapters, and Lydia Papadimitriou and Claire Molloy offered advice on various drafts of the book. Frank Krutnik, Warren Buckland and Peter Krämer gave valuable early criticisms on what eventually became Chapter 5. Rigas Goulimaris, Eleftheria Thanouli and Karen Ross engaged in many insightful discussions on the subject of film studies in general and American independent cinema in particular. Julia Hallam, a great friend and colleague, provided me with the ideal environment in which to pursue my scholarly interests in the School of Politics and Communication at the University of Liverpool.

My family and friends have supported me in numerous ways. I would especially like to thank my parents, Panayiotis and Christina Tzioumakis; Patroula Vrantza-Tzioumakis; Christina Tzioumakis; Panayiotis, Dimitra, Fenia and Ioanna Koutakis; Harris, Jason and Orestes Papadopoulos; Maria Goulimari; and Katerina Yanniki. I would also like to thank Frank Halligan; Sheena Streather; Julie Butler; Linda Crane; Paul Shaughnessy; Yolanda Akil-Perez; Adriana Shaughnessy-Akil; Lisa Anderson; Utpal Shah; Ben Howarth; Joanne Whiteside; Andy, Ruby and Esme Stockell; Alex Weir; Jim Friel; Roger and Maggie Lincoln; and Carys, Alex and James Damon. I wish to acknowledge the support and friendship of the late Paresh Lad.

I have taught *The Spanish Prisoner* in my module on American independent cinema for many years. At least 200 students have watched the film with me, many of whom made invaluable contributions in class discussions and influenced the approach this book has taken, especially Becky Thurston, Claire McGlasham and Dan Gage, who in the final year of their degree became my research assistants during this project.

Finally, there are two people who have exerted, for different reasons, the most influence on this book: Harris Tlas, with whom I have spent endless hours talking about confidence games and watching con artist and con game films and TV shows; and Siân Lincoln, who has embarked with me on this journey and whose love, devotion, understanding and support have guided me, especially through the writing stage of this project. Thanks so much to you both.

I am indebted to the *Velvet Light Trap* for allowing me to reproduce as Chapter 2 of this book a revised version of my essay: 'Marketing David Mamet: Institutionally Assigned Film Authorship and Contemporary American Cinema', which first appeared in *The Velvet Light Trap*, No. 57, Spring 2006, pp. 60–75. Copyright © 2006 by the University of Texas Press. All rights reserved.

For my brother,

Leonidas

For his love and support and for being my 'accomplice' in the appreciation of many 'indie' cinematic treasures over the years

Introduction: 'You don't know who anyone is'

Approximately eighteen minutes into *The Spanish Prisoner*, there are three scenes that involve Joe Ross, the corporate designer and inventor protagonist of the film, and Susan Ricci, the new company secretary and, to that point in the narrative, Joe's potential romantic interest. The scenes take place in the first class compartment of a plane flying back to New York from the Caribbean islands. It was there where Joe, Susan and a few select employees of a New York-based company had enjoyed a short stay on the company's account, while trying to pitch to a group of investors and businessmen Joe's invention – a mathematical formula through which a corporation could control the global market and which is referred to throughout the film as 'the process'. While on the island, Joe befriended a mysterious, well-off, middle-aged man named Julian 'Jimmy' Dell, with whom he made arrangements to meet in New York after agreeing to drop off to Dell's sister a package on his behalf.

The first of the three scenes opens with a shot of Joe in the plane corridor trying to find his seat. Susan and George Lang, Joe's business partner and company lawyer, follow him to their own seats. Noticing that Susan struggles to place her bags on the luggage compartment, Joe, who had earlier upgraded Susan's ticket from economy to first class, quickly volunteers to help her. Assuming that the 'colourful' Susan does not belong to the first class an air-stewardess enters the shot to check Susan's ticket. Susan explains to her that she would normally not travel first class and elaborates on Joe's gesture of arranging for her to sit 'in quality'. Prompted by the air-stewardess's check on her, Susan turns to Joe and utters: 'it shows you, you never know who anybody is', a phrase that marks the end of this rather long take and one that is destined to become a major motif for the rest of the film.

Joe nods agreeably to Susan's remark, which encourages Susan to repeat her earlier dictum once again, most probably to make conversation with him. She then dares Joe to guess the real profession of a woman they both met on the island, who had claimed she worked for the FBI. Rather uninterested but with nothing better to do, Joe decides to play Susan's game and admits he cannot guess the woman's profession, prompting Susan to reply emphatically that she *did* work for the FBI and to produce her business card as proof. Joe checks the card and hands it back to Susan while uttering the old cliché 'funny old world'. Susan takes the card back and offers the much more original adage, 'dog my cats', which the amused Joe decides to adopt as the appropriate conclusion to his verbal exchange with Susan. The scene ends with a close-up shot of the package Jimmy had asked Joe to deliver to his sister. Joe places the package in the pocket of the seat in front of him and fastens his seatbelt for the take off.

In the second scene – and via a dissolve – we are at a later stage of the flight. Joe is standing again in the corridor looking at some notes and drinking orange juice. As he starts walking towards his seat, he once again hears Susan uttering: 'You never know who anybody is.' Susan repeats the same phrase yet again, but this time exempts herself from the otherwise axiomatic dictum by arguing that she is what she looks like and therefore cannot be anyone else. Smiling, she continues: 'why is that Mr Ross?' Thinking that perhaps Susan is fishing for a compliment, Joe decides to give in and in his own nonchalant manner compliments Susan by telling her that she looks 'just fine'.

Susan, however, has not been fishing for compliments. Instead, she continues talking about deceptive appearances and brings to the conversation Jimmy Dell as an example of someone who might not be who he appeared to be. Slightly surprised and somewhat more interested in the conversation, Joe responds that Jimmy was 'a fellow who got off a plane', an answer which prompts Susan to question its status as a fact. In a rather playful manner, Joe tells Susan that she can't 'go on mistrusting every-one', which triggers Susan's more playful response, 'no, just strangers'. Joe decides to put an end to the chat by responding categorically that he saw Jimmy getting off the plane, a rather surprising statement as it does not prove in any way that Jimmy was not 'a stranger'.

Susan offers an alternative version of the event, however, namely that she and Joe saw him getting off a boat that came from the direction of the plane. Yet Joe remains adamant, insisting on having seen Jimmy getting off the plane, to which Susan responds: 'that's what you just think you saw'. To support her version of events, Susan reminds Joe of a picture she took of him on the island, in the background of which she saw

Jimmy getting off a boat. Deciding to finish off the conversation herself she returns to a paraphrased version of her dictum, 'we've no idea who anyone is', which by this time has been uttered at least five times, while in the background the air-stewardess starts distributing Customs forms to the passengers.

At this point there is a short verbal exchange between Joe and George about whether they should declare their Cuban cigars to Customs. In the next shot, however, Susan suddenly picks up the conversation where it was left and starts talking about 'mules', people who are handed packages by strangers and who might carry illegal material for people whom they do not know, people who trust strangers and get duped. She finishes this point by a slightly different rendition of her by that time harrowing phrase: 'who is what they seem? Who, in this world, is what they seem?' Joe's reaction is immediate. He realises that the hypothetical people Susan talks about could be him. He picks up the package from the pocket of the front seat, while non-diegetic music starts playing. He stops momentarily to reflect on what he will do, then gets up and walks towards the back of the plane, package in hand. The camera tracks in behind him as the air-stewardess asks him to return to his seat.

In the third scene of this sequence, Joe has refused to obey the air-stewardess and has locked himself in the toilet. With signs of anxiety evident in his face, he clumsily tears the wrapping paper, not knowing what to expect. It is with a sense of relief that he discovers that the suspect package was just a book about tennis sent by Jimmy to his sister, with an accompanying note in which Jimmy recommended Joe as a 'good fellow' and as someone appropriate for her to date. But in his rush and clumsiness Joe has also torn the front cover of the book, making it clear that he 'tampered' with a package given to him in good faith. Although this creates a new problem for him to solve, for the time Joe is happy to see that he has not been duped or used as a 'mule'.

Besides their significance in the construction of the narrative, which I shall address in later chapters, these scenes also represent an elegantly structured confidence game between Susan and Joe. If one accepts that a confidence game is an exchange between two parties where one uses persuasive techniques in order to convince the other to hand over willingly something desired by the first party, whether this is an object, money, information or anything else that might carry value for a particular person or group of people, then the verbal exchange between Joe and Susan has all the characteristics of a confidence trick.

In these scenes, Joe (and through him the spectator) is originally invited to construe the verbal exchange with Susan as casual conversation initiated by the female character, who in previous scenes was presented as romantically attracted to him. Certain about the nature of Susan's banter, Joe, who in previous scenes made clear to George Lang that he would not reciprocate, tries to ensure that the conversation remains casual through quick, agreeable responses to Susan's persistent questions and remarks. Even his one compliment to Susan – 'you look just fine' – is uttered in as matter-of-fact a manner as possible.

However, some of Joe's actions (upgrading Susan's ticket, helping her with her luggage, offering her a compliment and generally being courteous and agreeable to her within what seems to be a strictly hierarchical company environment) suggest that he enjoys Susan's attention, despite his lack of feelings for her.[1] One could argue, then, that Joe is 'playing' with Susan. Having perceived himself as the more powerful of the two, the one who is in control of the narrative situation, Joe cultivates in Susan's mind the possibility of romance or, to be more precise, does not entirely deny (at least in front of Susan) this possibility.

A key characteristic of a confidence game, though, is that in such a situation it is always the 'mark' who believes they are in control of any exchange or transaction between themselves and a second party, a belief that normally stems from their lack of awareness, even complete misconception, about their role in the exchange. Since there are only two people involved in these scenes, Joe and Susan, the question is who occupies the position of the con artist and who of the mark. The answer to this question seems obvious: the desired something for Joe is Susan's attention. On the basis of false pretences (the possibility of romance), Joe, who does not have a social life outside work, ensures that he is and will be Susan's object of attention and desire. This clearly makes Joe a con artist and Susan, who does not know that Joe does not intend to reciprocate, the victim of a con.

But the answer the narrative encourages at this point could not have been more misleading, as it becomes apparent in later scenes that it was Joe who was completely unaware of his part in the verbal exchange with Susan. Rather than being the 'harmless' con artist, swindling his way to Susan's attention, Joe turns out to be the mark of an extremely elaborate con game designed to make him hand over his exceptionally valuable invention. This con was perpetrated by a number of people, including Susan, with each person playing a particular part in their every exchange with him for the duration of the film. Susan's attention to Joe, therefore, which he thinks he has consciously encouraged, is in actual fact one of the tasks that Susan's role in the con entails. In the first two of the scenes on the plane, Susan's task is to raise Joe's suspicion about whether Jimmy Dell is someone Joe could trust. By relentlessly repeating that nobody ever knows who anyone is, Susan finally manages to direct the naïve Joe to her objective for that specific encounter, that is, to make him check that the package Jimmy gave him to deliver does not contain anything illegal. Joe is now certain that he can trust Dell, whose own part in the con will be to advise Joe in his capacity as a successful businessman on how to handle the company's lack of trust in him later in the narrative, and so on.

The emphasis on the 'invisible' con, which neither the protagonist nor the spectator is able to perceive until almost the final scenes of the film, as a structuring principle of the narrative of *The Spanish Prisoner* is one of the central features of the film. Review after review of the film highlighted Mamet's 'labyrinthine story development',[2] that 'the entire movie is one huge confidence trick'[3] and that 'Mamet outHitchcocks Hitchcock by stuffing the plot so full of McGuffins that the audience never quite knows who or what to trust.'[4]

Yet when it comes to identifying the film genre to which *The Spanish Prisoner* belongs, film reviewers tend to opt for either established labels such as the thriller, the film noir (or the neo-noir), the crime film and even recently critically accepted generic labels such as the puzzle film.[5] Alternatively, film reviewers find it difficult to pinpoint a particular film genre to which Mamet's film belongs and therefore resort to colloquial descriptive appellations such as 'ripping yarn'[6] and to comparisons with similarly themed or structured films, especially Hitchcock's *The 39 Steps* (1935) and *North by Northwest* (1959) and Bryan Singer's *The Usual Suspects* (1995).[7] This suggests that the central element of the confidence game is treated by the critical apparatus as a narrative feature and not as intrinsic to the film's generic status. In this respect, when it comes to questions of genre film critics seem to privilege other elements, such as the film's ability to thrill its audience through its wrongly accused protagonist on the run and the various twists and turns of the story, in addition to the dark, terse mood that formal elements such as the *mise en scène* and cinematography register.

One of the main objectives of this book is to redress this situation by introducing the terms 'con artist film' and 'con game film' as distinct generic labels that should be applied to *The Spanish Prisoner* and to an increasingly large number of films that deal with confidence men and women who ply their trade on unsuspected victims. Among others, such films would include: *The Sting* (G. R. Hill, 1973); *Paper Moon* (Bogdanovich, 1973); *The Sting II* (Kagan, 1983); *House of Games* (Mamet, 1987); *The Grifters* (Frears, 1990); *Traveller* (J. N. Green, 1997); *Catch Me If You Can* (Spielberg, 2002); *Confidence* (Foley, 2003); *Matchstick Men* (R. Scott, 2003); and *Criminal* (Jacobs, 2004). Specifically, the book will argue that such films are generically distinct from both crime films and thrillers and therefore labels such as the con artist film and the con game film (a subcategory of the con artist film) are more appropriate, and in the final analysis more useful, in approaching critically any of the above films.

More importantly, though, this book will examine *The Spanish Prisoner* within the context of contemporary American independent cinema. This is a context that almost all critical approaches to the film and to the body of the cinematic work of the film's director, David Mamet, have consistently ignored. And yet Mamet has had an illustrious career within the independent sector, with six out of his nine features to date as a writer-director produced and/or distributed within the confines of the 'indie' scene and in collaboration with such stalwarts of American independent cinema as Orion Pictures (financer and distributor of his debut *House of Games*), Triumph Releasing Corporation (distributor of *Homicide*, 1991), and the Samuel Goldwyn Company (co-financer and distributor of *Oleanna*, 1994).

Commencing from the position that Mamet was allowed to develop his own cinematic practice and to stamp on all his films a very distinctive aesthetic vision because of his early association with independent film companies,[8] the book will offer an in-depth examination of *The Spanish Prisoner* as both an example of a 'Mamet film', and, more importantly, a characteristic example of an 'indie' film during a transitional period in the history of American independent cinema. In terms of the first objective, the book will account for the plethora of stylistic and narrative peculiarities of the film, many of which can be construed as instances of an authorial signature, which locate the film firmly in the periphery of Hollywood cinema, despite its crowd-pleasing subject and the presence of star performers like Steve Martin.

This approach will complement the book's other objective, namely to provide a comprehensive view of American independent cinema at the end of the twentieth century, a time when the term 'independent cinema' started coming under direct questioning from the critical establishment, and other alternative labels, such as 'indie' (short for 'independent' but also signifying a film that could have been produced and/or distributed by major independents, mini-majors or classics divisions of major studios such as Sony Pictures Classics), became more dominant.[9] The practising of 'indie' cinema by filmmakers associated with companies integrated into the structures of conglomerate media and finance changed the industrial structure of the American independent cinema scene in fundamental ways and transformed this mode of filmmaking from a grassroots movement to a firmly institutionalised category. It is within this framework that *The Spanish Prisoner* can be seen as a key example of contemporary American 'indie' cinema, which, as I shall argue, should be perceived as different from 'independent' cinema.

The first chapter, then, entitled 'From Independent to "Indie" Cinema', will provide an overview of the independent sector in the late 1990s. It will pay particular attention to what I call the emergence of the 'third wave of classics divisions', companies like Fox Searchlight, Paramount Classics, Focus Features and Warner Independent Pictures. These subsidiaries of the conglomerates that control the global entertainment industry were established with the explicit intention of claiming a slice of the blossoming independent market. Not surprisingly, with companies like Fox, Universal and Warner behind them, this new wave of classics divisions became an instant force in the market, reshaping and redefining it, especially in terms of the level of funds available for production and marketing costs of 'low-budget' films. As a result, established independent distributors like October Films and older classics divisions like Sony Pictures Classics and Fine Line Features started distributing more 'upmarket' films with more potential for commercial success than other types of films. With the third wave of classics divisions controlling the market alongside major independents like Miramax, the label 'independent' had lost its exegetic power. The label 'indie' became a much used (and arguably useful) substitute to define the more commercial type of film that this new industrial configuration made possible.

Following this overview, Chapter 2 examines David Mamet as an 'indie' filmmaker. Often referred to as one of the most important playwrights in the history of American stage, and author of now classic plays such as *American Buffalo* (1976), *Glengarry Glen Ross* (1984) and *Oleanna* (1992), Mamet soon turned to cinema as a screenwriter of major films such as *The Postman Always Rings Twice* (Rafelson, 1981), *The Verdict*

(Lumet, 1982) and *The Untouchables* (De Palma, 1987). When Mamet decided to make the leap to behind the camera, though, he found that the majors were reluctant to allow him to make his films according to his very specific aesthetic vision. He eventually made his first film, *House of Games*, for Orion Pictures, the quintessential independent film production and distribution company of the 1980s. In subsequent years, Mamet reduced his playwriting and screenwriting for hire to a considerable extent while establishing a sustained career a writer-director.

Interestingly, between 1993 and 2001, Mamet severed his ties with mainstream Hollywood and gradually emerged as a director-brand name for the 'indie' sector, making a particular, instantly recognisable type of film that distributors like the Samuel Goldwyn Company, Sony Pictures Classics and Fine Line Features felt they could market effectively to a niche audience. The chapter discusses the major thematic, aesthetic and philosophical characteristics of Mamet's filmmaking and explores the manner in which the filmmaker's often difficult films have been marketed to a particular audience, one which understands what the phrase 'a David Mamet film' means.

With the characteristics of contemporary 'indie' cinema and of Mamet's work established, the book then commences its detailed examination of *The Spanish Prisoner*. Chapter 3 focuses on the industrial location of the film. After an account of Jean Doumanian Productions and Sweetland Films, which co-produced the film, the chapter moves to a comprehensive discussion of Sony Pictures Classics and of its role in making *The Spanish Prisoner* the most commercially successful film in the specialty market for 1998, a market for low-budget American 'indies' and non-US arthouse films. Having established a reputation for marketing successfully an unusually large number of arthouse non-US films, including *Farinelli* (Corbiau, 1994) and *La Cité des enfants perdus* [*The City of Lost Children*] (Caro and Jeunet, 1995), and a small but increasing number of 'homegrown indie' films like *Amateur* (Hartley, 1995) and *Safe* (Haynes, 1996), Sony Pictures Classics treated Mamet's film as a textbook 'indie' film. The marketing of the film as a 'Mamet creation', the film's participation and success in the Sundance Film Festival, and the further emphasis on the film's generic status as a con game film in the marketing campaign succeeded in creating a particular 'identity' which brought in record audiences for a Mamet film.

On the other hand, though, this identity failed to pronounce the film's (and Mamet's) signature stylistic and aesthetic traits, which have made his films instantly recognisable for fans of his work and have helped situate them at the periphery of Hollywood. Chapter 4 discusses these traits by offering a detailed examination of the distinctive use of visual style and of the several peculiarities in the construction of the film's narrative. Specifically, it argues that both narrative and film style depart, often drastically, from established Hollywood cinema norms, to the extent that the film's overall aesthetic is markedly different from dominant aesthetic paradigms in mainstream American cinema, especially from what film scholars have labelled as the classical aesthetic.

As analysis of key scenes from the film will demonstrate, although the narrative structure in *The Spanish Prisoner* follows the central tenets of classical narrative (causal, spatial and temporal coherence, continuity and psychological character motivation), on several occasions the narrative rids itself of such traits and follows a logic of its own. As a result, the story tends to become highly implausible and therefore problematic for spectators who are used to the rules of classical storytelling and whose main pleasure from American cinema comes from attending the unfolding of a 'good' story. Equally, the film's visual style tends to follow the rules of classical filmmaking by being at the service of the narrative, though it also breaks those rules on numerous occasions. These breaks take various forms but become particularly prominent when, in a rather forceful manner, the camera tries to provide for the benefit of the spectator 'clues' about the unfolding of the confidence game. The result is a peculiar hybrid of a visual style that is functional (i.e. at the service of the narrative) but which also comments on the narrative and breaks the spectator's engagement with the story in ways that a classical style would never do.

Finally, Chapter 5 is dedicated to the problem of genre that opened this introduction. It will introduce the genre labels 'con artist film' and 'con game film' and will discuss *The Spanish Prisoner* as a definitive example of the 'con game film'. This generic label, which should also be attached to *House of Games*, *Matchstick Men* and *Criminal*, is primarily characterised by the narrative's emphasis on the victim as the protagonist of the film and point of identification for the spectator, the 'invisible' structuring of the narrative by the confidence game, and a more forceful subversion of spectators' expectations than in the con artist film. As a result *The Spanish Prisoner* differs substantially from films like *The Sting*, *The Grifters* and *Confidence*, which adopt the perspective of con artists and where the spectator tends to be aware of the con artists' plans from the beginning.

The book will conclude with a brief epilogue about the film's contested independent status and will argue that even in the increasingly commercialised and institutionalised American independent cinema landscape of the mid-to-late 1990s, it was indeed possible for a filmmaker with a distinctive and often 'uncommercial' aesthetic view to continue to make films according to his or her own vision. Mamet remains a unique voice in American cinema, and the book will argue that it is his association with the independent sector that made this possible.

1. From Independent to 'Indie' Cinema

Introduction: The Golden Years

In 1996, a year before the release of *The Spanish Prisoner*, film industry analysts and critics proclaimed enthusiastically that that was 'the year of the independents'.[1] At first sight, such a proclamation seemed surprising, given that the hit films of the year were all from the conglomerated Hollywood majors. Fox was responsible for the biggest commercial success of 1996, the extremely popular (and in our case ironically titled) *Independence Day* (Emmerich), which recorded worldwide grosses of $811.4 million from its cinema release, of which $306.1 million was in the North American market. Warner followed at some distance with *Twister* (de Bont), the global cinema box office of which was $493.6 million, with $241.7 made in the US and Canada markets, while Paramount was a close third with *Mission Impossible* (De Palma), with global box-office takings of $464.9 million, $284 million of which was in the domestic market.[2]

On a closer look, however, and beyond the top three in terms of box-office receipts, the proclamation 'the year of the independents' seemed to have considerable merit, as evidence of a maturing American independent cinema sector was certainly in abundance. For instance, according to an annual industry survey, export revenues for the 130 independent film companies represented by the American Film Marketing Association peaked at $1.65 billion in 1996. Almost a third of these revenues ($501 million) stemmed from worldwide cinema distribution rights – a 37 per cent increase from 1995 – while an impressive $736 million represented revenues generated from the licensing of their films to television – an 11 per cent increase on the previous year.[3]

At the same time, small independent distributors (like October and the Samuel Goldwyn Company), major independent companies (like Miramax and New Line Cinema), classics divisions of the major conglomerates (like Sony Picture Classics and Fox Searchlight) and 'neo-indies' (companies partly owned by the majors, like Castle Rock) were paying increasingly large amounts of money to secure distribution rights to independently produced films screened in festivals like the Sundance Film Festival and the Toronto International Film Festival, and in annual industry showcases such as the Independent Film Project Market.

Led by Miramax, whose aggressive marketing campaigns had turned low-budget films like *sex, lies and videotape* (Soderbergh, 1989) and *The Crying Game* (Jordan, 1992) into spectacular money-earners and the company into the market leader in the sector, especially after its corporate takeover by Disney in 1993, distribution companies from across the 'independent spectrum' upped their acquisition rights budgets dramatically in order to compete with Miramax. Thus, while an early independent film of the 1980s, like *Return of the Secaucus Seven* (Sayles, 1980), was purchased by small independent distributor Libra Films for an advance of just $25,000,[4] by 1996 Miramax would spend $5 million to acquire the distribution rights of *Swingers* (Liman),[5] while Castle Rock would spend an astounding $10 million – the highest amount ever paid for an acquisition of an independent film to 1996 – to secure worldwide distribution rights for *The Spitfire Grill* (Zlotoff), winner of the Audience Award at the 1996 Sundance Film Festival.[6]

News from the festivals front kept getting better and better. Submissions to the Sundance Film Festival had been increasing exponentially over the years, from 60 submissions in 1987 to over 600 in 1996.[7] Slamdance, a second film festival running concurrently with Sundance in Park City, Utah, to accommodate the hordes of independent films that were produced and not getting accepted in Sundance, was in its second year after a successful launch in 1995. Other festivals, like the Toronto International Film Festival and the Telluride Film Festival in Berkeley, California, were also blossoming, becoming major platforms for the showcasing of independent films. Similarly, film festivals in Europe, once reserved for films by world cinema auteurs and a few prestigious American productions, had also become major destinations for American independent films, especially when films of that designation won the major awards in the Cannes Film Festival three years in a row (*sex, lies and videotape* [1989], *Wild at Heart* [Lynch, 1990] and *Barton Fink* [Joel and Ethan Coen, 1991]). Alongside Cannes, Venice and Thessaloniki became significant hubs for the visibility of American independent cinema, while newly established festivals also joined forces in showcasing independent cinema, with the Austin Film

Festival in Texas (launched in 1994) and the Heartland Film Festival in Indianapolis (launched in 1991) attracting considerable attention.

The year 1996 also saw the launch of the Sundance Channel, 'the television destination for independent-minded viewers seeking something different',[8] and an additional exhibition outlet for independent films. Indiewire, 'a daily news service for independent film',[9] was launched on 15 July of the same year as an email publication and then steadily grew into one of the pillars of institutional support for independent filmmaking. At the US box office, independent film was making its presence strongly felt with an increasing number of films casually smashing the $10 million mark in grosses – an unattainable target not so long before 1996. *Big Night*, *Fargo*, *Flirting with Disaster*, *From Dusk Till Dawn*, *Lone Star*, *Sling Blade* and *The Spitfire Grill* all grossed over $10 million, with *Fargo* and *Sling Blade* approaching the $25 million mark and *From Dusk Till Dawn* passing it in box-office gross in the US alone.[10] This meant that independent films were achieving increasing visibility, as in order for a film to break the $10 million barrier, it needed to play not only in the small arthouse screens dedicated to low-budget features but also in the major multiplexes that attract the majority of paying customers.[11]

Furthermore, these films could now also benefit from cinema releases in international markets, once nothing short of a dream for almost all independent filmmakers. With distributors like Miramax establishing links with local distribution companies in various territories, like Spentzos Films in Greece, and with new distribution companies established in the early-to-mid-1990s around the world to exploit audience demand for independent films, like Scanbox Entertainment in Finland (originally a home entertainment distributor which branched out to cinema distribution in 1996 with *Bound* [Andy and Larry Wachowski] and gradually became the main distributor of American independent films in Finland), international cinema exhibition became an important stream of revenue for independent films.

The year 1996 also saw a large number of established filmmakers firmly associated with the independent sector returning with new films: John Sayles with *Lone Star*, Abel Ferrara with *The Funeral*, Joel and Ethan Coen with *Fargo*, Jim Jarmusch with *Dead Man*, David O. Russell with *Flirting with Disaster*, Spike Lee with *Girl 6*, Allison Anders with *Grace of My Heart*, Robert Rodriguez with *From Dusk Till Dawn* and Richard Linklater with *SubUrbia*. At the other end, new filmmakers like Mary Harron (*I Shot Andy Warhol*), Doug Liman (*Swingers*), Steve Buscemi (*Trees Lounge*), Andy and Larry Wachowski (*Bound*) and Alexander Payne (*Citizen Ruth*) made significant 'buzz' with their debut films, irrespective of their unspectacular and often poor cinema box office. Table 1.1 summarises activity in the independent sector in 1996, as it presents an indicative list of the key independent films released in that year, their distributors, the festivals they participated in and their gross at the US box office.[12]

Arguably the greatest piece of evidence to suggest that 1996 was, indeed, 'the year of the independents' came on the morning of 11 February 1997 when the nominations for the 69th Academy Awards were announced. The list of nominations included a record fourteen films that carried the 'independent' label, a label that in this case also included all films in the English language made outside the US, like Australian production *Shine* (Hicks) and British production *Secrets and Lies* (Leigh), and released by American distributors other than the majors, which at that time consisted of Paramount, Buena Vista, Columbia/TriStar, Universal, Warner, Fox and MGM.[13] Among them, these fourteen films received a record forty-four nominations and represented six marginal distribution companies alongside specialist market leader Miramax, which received the lion's share with eighteen out of those forty-four nominations, as Table 1.2 demonstrates.

Crucially, four out of these fourteen independent films (*The English Patient* [Minghella], *Fargo*, *Secrets and Lies* and *Shine*) featured in the all-important Best Picture category, with *Jerry Maguire* (Crowe), the fifth film in the category, being the only one financed and distributed by a Hollywood major.

Irrespective of the stretch of the definition of the label 'independent', which I will discuss shortly, the list of the Academy Awards nominations for the 1996 season is a good indicator of the shifting balance between the companies associated with the independent sector (independents, major independents, classics divisions) and the majors. While in previous years independent films always found their way to the Oscars, this was mostly the case for a handful of productions per year which garnered a small number of nominations in specific categories, especially acting and screenwriting. For instance, in 1985, independent films *Runaway Train* (Konchalovsky), *Kiss of the Spider Woman* (Babenco), *The Trip to Bountiful* (Masterson), *Twice in A Lifetime* (Yorkin) and *Broken Rainbow* (Mudd), alongside Orion Pictures' *Remo Williams: The Adventure Begins* (G. Hamilton) and *The Purple Rose of Cairo* (Woody Allen), received thirteen nominations among them and represented the efforts of six different small distributors.

Table 1.1 Independent films in 1996

Film	Director	Distributor	Festival	US box office
Basquiat	Julian Schnabel	Miramax		$3 m
Big Night	Campbell Scott and Stanley Tucci	Samuel Goldwyn Company	Toronto, Sundance	$12 m
Bound	Andy and Larry Wachowski	Gramercy	Toronto, Venice	$3.8 m
Citizen Ruth	Alexander Payne	Miramax and New Films International	Sundance, Thessaloniki	$0.15 m
Dead Man	Jim Jarmusch	Miramax	Cannes	$1 m
Fargo	Joel and Ethan Coen	Gramercy	Cannes	$24.6 m
Flirting with Disaster	David O. Russell	Miramax	Cannes	$14.8 m
Freeway	Matthew Bright	Roxie Releasing	Sundance	$0.3 m
From Dusk Till Dawn	Robert Rodriguez	Miramax		$25.7 m
Funeral	Abel Ferrara	October	Toronto, Venice	$1.2 m
Girl 6	Spike Lee	Fox Searchlight	Cannes	$5 m
Grace of My Heart	Allison Anders	Gramercy	Toronto	$0.6 m
I Shot Andy Warhol	Mary Harron	Samuel Goldwyn Company	Sundance, Cannes	$1.8 m
Lone Star	John Sayles	Sony Pictures Classics		$13.3 m
Looking for Richard	Al Pacino	Fox Searchlight	Toronto	$1.3 m
Schizopolis	Steven Soderbergh	Wellspring Media	Toronto	$0.01 m
Sling Blade	Billy Bob Thornton	Miramax	Telluride, New York, Austin	$24.5 m
Spitfire Grill	Steven Zlotoff	Castle Rock	Sundance	$12.6 m
Suburbia	Richard Linklater	Sony Pictures Classics	New York Film Festival	$0.5 m
Swingers	Doug Liman	Miramax	Venice, Toronto	$4.5 m
Trees Lounge	Steve Buscemi	Orion Classics	Toronto	$0.6 m
Unhook the Stars	Nick Cassavetes	Miramax	Toronto	$0.25 m
Walking and Talking	Nicole Holofcener	Miramax	Sundance	$1.2 m

Table 1.2 Indies at the 1996 Oscars

Distributor	Nominations	Films
Miramax	18	*The English Patient* (12) *Marvin's Room* (1) *Emma* (2) *Trainspotting* (1) *Sling Blade* (2)
Gramercy	10	*Fargo* (7) *Portrait of a Lady* (2) *When We Were Kings* (1)
Fine Line Features	7	*Shine* (7)
October	6	*Secrets and Lies* (5) *Breaking the Waves* (1)
Samuel Goldwyn Company	1	*Angels and Insects* (1)
Castle Hills Productions	1	*The Line King: The Al Hirschfeld Story* (1)
Sony Pictures Classics	1	*Lone Star* (1)
7 distributors	44 nominations	14 films

Equally, in 1989, another year that is widely considered to be important in the history of the independent sector, non-Hollywood productions *Henry V* (Branagh), *sex, lies and videotape, My Left Foot* (Sheridan), the documentary *Common Threads* (Epstein and Friedman) and Orion Pictures' *Crimes and Misdemeanors* (Woody Allen) and *Valmont* (Forman) had represented a particularly good crop, with fourteen nominations in total for four independent distribution companies. Yet no more than two independent films made it to the list of Best Picture category in each case (*Henry V* and *My Left Foot* in 1989; *Kiss of the Spider Woman* in 1985).

In the 1990s, however, the number of nominations started to increase as did the number of distribution companies associated with the independent sector. For instance, 1994 saw thirteen independent productions (including the ultra-commercial *Pulp Fiction* [Tarantino] and other well-known titles like *The Madness of King George III* [Hytner], *Bullets over Broadway* [Woody Allen], and the documentary *Hoop Dreams* [Steve James]) receiving thirty-one nominations and representing nine distributors. Miramax, which had already become a major force in the sector, led the way with four nominated films and seventeen nominations in total (with *Tom and Viv* [B. Gilbert] and *Heavenly Creatures* [Peter Jackson]

Table 1.3 The majors at the 1996 Oscars

Distributor	Nominations	Films
Buena Vista	10	*Evita* (5)
		The Rock (1)
		Up Close and Personal (1)
		The Hunchback of Notre Dame (1)
		James and the Giant Peach (1)
		The Preacher's Wife (1)
Columbia	9	*Hamlet* (4)
		Ghosts of Mississippi (2)
		Fly Away Home (1)
		The People versus Larry Flynt (2)
Fox	7	*Independence Day* (2)
		The Crucible (2)
		One Fine Day (1)
		William Shakespeare's Romeo and Juliet (1)
		That Thing You Do (1)
Warner	6	*Twister* (2)
		Eraser (1)
		Michael Collins (2)
		Sleepers (1)
TriStar	5	*Jerry Maguire* (4)
		The Mirror Has Two Faces (1)
Paramount	4	*The Ghost and the Darkness* (1)
		Star Trek: First Contact (1)
		The First Wives Club (1)
		Primal Fear (1)
Universal	3	*Dragonheart* (1)
		Daylight (1)
		The Nutty Professor (1)
MGM	1	*The Birdcage* (1)
8 distributors	45 nominations	29 films

being the other two films next to *Pulp Fiction* and *Bullets over Broadway* that represented the company that year). In this respect, the fourteen nominated films, the forty-four nominations but mostly the four Best Picture nominations of 1996 were not a fluke. They were the result of a well-established trend under way since the early 1990s.

Although the major studios had an almost identical number of nominations in 1996 (forty-five nominations for eight distribution companies), these nominations were spread out over a much larger group of films (twenty-nine films in total, as Table 1.3 demonstrates). Furthermore, the majority of these nominations were in secondary, technical award categories that rarely register with the wide cinema-going public. On the evening of the Oscar ceremony, the independent companies found themselves victorious in fifteen categories, with Miramax's *The English Patient* winning nine Oscars, leaving only the Actor in a Supporting Role, Achievement in Make Up, Achievement in Music (Original Song), Achievement in Sound Editing, and Achievement in Visual Effects categories to be won by the majors' films.

This undisputed success of independent films in 1996 can be seen as representative of a particularly prosperous period for the independent sector in the mid-to-late 1990s. This period was characterised by increased economic opportunities following the sluggish economic environment of the late 1980s/early 1990s, when banks had kept credit borrowing in check. The strong market of the latter part of the 1990s meant that financial institutions were now more willing to provide independent filmmakers with funds as the chances of making a profit were considerably increased.[14] Furthermore, independent film production found a significant source of funding in the European terrestrial television market. By pre-selling television rights to an increasing number of television stations around Europe which were hungry for cheap product, independent filmmakers tapped into an additional source of income which remained significant until the end of the decade.[15] With finance available from a variety of sources and with demand for product running high, especially as the market had become increasingly global and new streams of revenue had convinced investors that independent production was a potentially lucrative proposition, the second half of the 1990s arguably represented the golden years of American independent cinema.

However, by that time the whole edifice of independent cinema had changed dramatically, especially compared to the independent sector during the early 1980s, when commercial independent filmmaking had first emerged as a sustainable alternative mode of film practice to Hollywood cinema. If independent cinema in the 1980s was largely 'a trust-fund enterprise',[16] occasionally supported by small federal grants and donations made by the filmmakers' families and friends, and exemplified by films like *Return of the Secaucus Seven*, *Smithereens* (Seidelman, 1982) and *Stranger than Paradise* (Jarmusch, 1984), this was certainly not the case for independent cinema in the latter part of the 1990s.

The Problem of the Classics Divisions

By the mid-1990s, independent cinema had become a multimillion-dollar business with a vast institutional apparatus promoting and supporting it, while key independent titles would include multimillion-dollar productions featuring a number of stars, like *Jackie Brown* (Tarantino, 1997), *Good Will Hunting* (Van Sant, 1997) and *Shakespeare in Love* (Madden, 1998). In the words of Christine Vachon, producer of many famous independent films in the early 1990s, like *Poison* (Haynes, 1991) and *Swoon* (Kalin, 1992), the perception of what independent cinema was had changed to such an extent after the mid-1990s that it affected film-goers' expectations: 'When they go to see a so-called independent film they want to see *Shakespeare in Love*, they don't want to see something that is really challenging, that's in black and white, where the sound is difficult to make out.'[17]

If nothing else, these developments clearly suggest that the label 'independent' had also become relative. While for most of the 1980s and the early 1990s the label was (wrongly) employed without questions or objections, as it had yet to acquire an added value, from the mid-1990s onwards it came to represent an increasingly loosely defined type of film, and not necessarily a production made outside the influence of mainstream Hollywood cinema as this was represented by the practices of the conglomerated majors. Central to the problem was that during the 1980s and early 1990s it was relatively easy to determine who the practitioners of independent filmmaking were, as there were three main types of distributors in the industry and two of them were clearly in the business of independent cinema. The three types of distributors were:

- the conglomerated majors: interested mainly in event films and star vehicles that target the widest possible audience and bring more profit from merchandising and ancillary markets sales than from cinema admissions;
- the independents: distribution companies with no corporate ties or affiliations with the majors, which bought the rights of low-budget, independently produced films and marketed them to distinct niche audiences; and
- the classics divisions: small subsidiaries of the majors that were originally established to distribute non-American films in the North

American market but which gradually started distributing a small number of independently produced and financed American films, in effect competing with the independents.[18]

Despite the potential problem that the third type of distributor raised, the classics divisions' corporate ties with the major conglomerates did not become a contentious issue in the 1980s, as the classics remained strictly in the distribution business, rarely attempting to finance or produce films. This means that companies like United Artists Classics, Universal Classics, 20th Century Fox International Classics, Triumph Films (Columbia's classics division in the 1980s) and Orion Classics – which constitute the first wave of classics divisions – were allocated an acquisitions and marketing budget from their respective parent companies to conduct business but were not allowed to tap into the parent companies' resources to finance production or to outmuscle competition from independent distributors.

Furthermore, their emphasis was largely on non-US films, which means that their volume of business with the American independent cinema sector was low. As a result, the operation costs of the classics divisions were minimal, while profits remained firmly below the $1 million mark. According to Mike Medavoy, head of worldwide production at Orion Pictures 1978–90, the most successful classics division of the second half of the 1980s, Orion Classics, never recorded profits of more than $600,000–700,000 per annum.[19] For that reason, such divisions tended to operate with great autonomy as long as they maintained profitability and were never considered an extension of the corporate parent.

With the exception of United Artists Classics, which dominated the early 1980s, and Orion Classics, which dominated the second half of the decade and the early 1990s, the classics divisions were short-lived experiments initiated by the majors in an effort to emulate the above two companies. Those released some of the key independent titles of the 1980s, such as *Lianna* (Sayles, 1983) and *Streamers* (Altman, 1983) for United Artists Classics and *Mystery Train* (Jarmusch, 1989) and *Slacker* (Linklater, 1991) for Orion Classics.

However, if the relationship of the first wave of the classics divisions to the American independent cinema sector was relatively minor and uncomplicated, this was not the case with the other two waves of classics divisions that followed in the 1990s. In 1991 and 1992 New Line Cinema, a well-established independent, and Sony Pictures, a major distributor, each formed a classics division: Fine Line Features and Sony

Pictures Classics, respectively. The latter seemed to be in the mould of the 1980s classics divisions, established to distribute non-US films in the North American market. As a matter of fact, Sony's new division was even headed by the same executives who previously ran Orion Classics (and before that United Artists Classics) and who changed jobs when Orion Classics' parent company, Orion Pictures, filed for bankruptcy in December 1991. Indeed, in its first three years of operation (1992–4) Sony Pictures Classics distributed twenty-one films, only two of them American (*Mi vida loca* [Anders] and *Vanya on 42nd Street* [Malle]). From 1995, however, the number of acquisitions of American films started increasing substantially: eight out of seventeen releases in 1995; eight out of thirteen releases in 1996; six out of twelve releases in 1997; and six out of eighteen releases in 1998.[20]

Fine Line Features, on the other hand, made it clear that it was established to exploit the emerging American independent cinema market, at a time when its parent company, New Line Cinema, was increasingly moving towards the production of genre star vehicles and franchise films. Fine Line's initial release slate for 1991 included five films, three of which were American productions, including celebrated independent films such as Gus Van Sant's *My Own Private Idaho*, Michael Tolkin's *The Rupture* and Hal Hartley's *Trust*. The following year Fine Line distributed thirteen films of which seven were American productions, and this ratio remained stable in the next few years (six out of eleven releases in 1993; seven out of ten releases in 1994).[21]

However, neither Sony Pictures Classics nor Fine Line remained strictly in the distribution business, as both companies ventured into the areas of film finance and production. Although such arrangements were relatively few (especially for Sony Pictures Classics) and were always in conjunction with other partners (especially the filmmakers themselves), this none the less meant that there existed a number of films associated strongly with the independent sector which were produced with money from a conglomerated major's subsidiary.[22] And even though Sony Pictures Classics's association with films like *The Celluloid Closet* (Russo, 1995), *Waiting for Guffman* (Guest, 1996) or *The Myth of Fingerprints* (Freundlich, 1997) as a co-producer did not necessarily mean that it influenced the production of those films, it did mark the beginning of a new era in American independent cinema, when the label 'independent' ceased to signify economic independence from the majors and instead became a signifier of a particular type of film, the 'indie' film. This was the era of American 'indie' cinema, which therefore needs to be seen as an extension and continuation of the American independent cinema of the 1980s and early 1990s.

While Sony Pictures Classics remained marginal in film finance and production, and Fine Line, despite its considerable production activity, was still a subsidiary of the independent New Line Cinema and therefore not part of conglomerated Hollywood, in the two-year period 1993–4 the landscape of independent cinema was subjected to seismic changes. In 1994 New Line Cinema ceased to be independent, as it was taken over by Turner Broadcasting System (TBS), a media conglomerate with stakes in cable networks such as CNN and Turner Classic Movies (while two years later, in 1996, and after a merger between TBS and Time Warner, New Line and Fine Line found themselves to be parts of the then largest conglomerated major). More importantly, a few months earlier (in May 1993) Miramax, the company most heavily associated by the cinema-going public with the distribution of American independent films, was taken over by Disney. If nothing else, these takeovers demonstrated that the Hollywood majors were taking seriously developments in the independent cinema sector, especially the fact that an increasing number of low-budget films were finding substantial commercial success, as my earlier discussion of the 1996 output clearly suggested.

The corporate takeovers of the two most established independent companies by Hollywood conglomerates created a new breed of film company, 'a curious hybrid', which Justin Wyatt called 'the major independent',[23] and which, arguably, transformed them into a new model of a classics division. Although both New Line Cinema and Miramax had been able to maintain a consistent market presence as independents, their respective takeovers gave them (especially Miramax) seemingly limitless access to funds in order to dominate the American independent cinema sector as well as 'more latitude in production decisions'.[24] Thus, while Miramax had already become a market leader with the commercial success of *sex, lies and videotape*, *My Left Foot* and *The Crying Game* and as early as 1991 was commanding revenues of $74.09 million and profits of $4.35 million,[25] four years after its takeover and with Disney's back-up it was able to co-finance films like *Good Will Hunting* and to reap the benefits of the film's $138 million gross in the North American market alone.[26] Additionally, Miramax was able to participate through a number of deals in the production process of a great number of films associated with the independent sector, such as *Pulp Fiction*, *Smoke*

(Wang, 1995) and *Flirting with Disaster*. As a result, the company was able to dominate the low-budget market while also co-producing and distributing more upmarket films that often became big crossover successes, as in the case of *Good Will Hunting* and of *The English Patient*.

New Line Cinema, on the other hand, moved towards genre films and star vehicles of considerably higher budgets than during its independent days, while Fine Line continued to operate with modest budgets and in the same market as before the takeover but with the security of backing by Turner and Warner (after 1996). Thus while New Line Cinema could gamble on expensive films like *Seven* (Fincher, 1995) and *The Long Kiss Goodnight* (Harlin, 1996), Fine Line could invest in the production of Robert Altman's *Kansas City* (1996) and Harmony Korine's notorious film *Gummo* (1997).

The changes in the independent sector that were put in motion by the corporate takeovers of New Line Cinema and Miramax were complemented by a new wave of classics divisions, which this time were established with the explicit intention of claiming a share of the emerging 'indie' market. Unlike Sony Pictures Classics and Fine Line, which remained relatively marginal in the film finance and production arenas and which distributed a mixture of homegrown and foreign arthouse films, the new classics divisions were characterised by equal emphasis on production and distribution of relatively low-budget American films, only occasionally venturing into distributing non-US fare. The company that initiated this phenomenon was Fox Searchlight, which was established in 1994 but which became active in the market only in late 1995 with the distribution of Ed Burns's Sundance-winning film *The Brothers McMullen*. Fox Searchlight consciously clouded the waters regarding the use of the 'independent' label, as it conceived of itself as an independent company. As its website states:

Established in 1994 as the **independent arm** of Twentieth Century Fox, Fox Searchlight Pictures is a filmmaker-oriented company, creating distinctive films helmed by **world-class auteurs** and **exciting newcomers**. By blending specialty releases with trademark arthouse fare, Fox Searchlight's leadership has solidified its position in the **independent film marketplace**. (original emphasis)[27]

Fox Searchlight's status allows it to finance upmarket productions with stars, such as Ang Lee's *Ice Storm* (1997) and Philip Kaufman's *Quills* (2000), while also taking gambles with less commercial titles like *Boys*

Don't Cry (Peirce, 1999) and *Waking Life* (Linklater, 2001). As one of the company's executives explained: 'having a strong parent company with deep pockets offers a certain amount of freedom, not only in making decisions about what to spend to acquire a film but also in determining how much money to devote to marketing costs'.[28] This means that Fox Searchlight can and will utilise 20th Century Fox's resources, especially when it handles upmarket productions with international stars that compete against studio star vehicles.

For instance, when Fox Searchlight understood that its film *Antwone Fisher* (D. Washington, 2002) had a potential for substantial commercial success, after a two-week limited release with impressive financial results, it relied on the parent company to supply the extra advertising costs necessary to open the film nationwide. Equally, for the genre picture *The Banger Sisters* (Dolman, 2002), 20th Century Fox assisted its subsidiary in opening the film in a massive 2,738 screens.[29] Tom Rothman, 20th Century Fox co-chairman, summarised the benefits of being this type of a classics division in contemporary American cinema:

It's not just the ability to take pictures wide, like *Antwone Fisher* and *The Banger Sisters*. It's also that there is a globally integrated campaign for movies. We're the only specialty company that doesn't have to go begging territory by territory . . . [Fox Searchlight] has the best of both worlds. That is, the risk-taking and flexibility of a specialty label and the power, leverage and scope of a major studio.[30]

This type of organisation, structure and positioning in the marketplace placed Fox Searchlight in direct competition with Miramax, while its dual emphasis on production and distribution of upmarket films, and on the distribution of riskier low-budget productions, allowed the company also to compete against New Line Cinema and Fine Line Features at the same time. Although Fox Searchlight did not initially record the same box-office success as Miramax, it none the less saw a small number of its low-budget releases becoming box-office champions, like *The Brothers McMullen* and British production *The Full Monty* (Cataneo, 1997), which helped maintain the company's profitability despite several flops such as *Blood and Wine* (Rafelson, 1996) and *Waking Ned* (Kirk Jones, 1998).

The Fox Searchlight experiment convinced the rest of the conglomerated majors that the time was ripe for a new influx of classics divisions which would concentrate primarily on the American 'indie' market as both producers and distributors, while occasionally looking outside the

US for arthouse films in other languages that had the potential for a breakthrough success with the American cinema-going public. The fact that the time was right became even clearer in the 1998–9 season, when the controversial Italian film *La Vita è bella* ([*Life is Beautiful*], Benigni, 1997) became an unprecedented commercial hit for Miramax, grossing over $57.5 million at the US box office.[31]

Paramount Classics (now Paramount Vantage) was the first one to follow Fox Searchlight. Paramount Classics was set up in 1998 to 'seek low-cost pics that can generate enough biz on the arthouse circuit to stay in the black', though in recent years it has focused on films that are 'riskier, more creative and aimed at a younger demo'.[32] The company's early hits were *The Virgin Suicides* (S. Coppola, 1999) and especially *You Can Count On Me* (Lonergan, 2000). Sony followed a year later with its second classics division, Screen Gems. As Sony Pictures Classics was more of an old-style classics arm specialising in art films acquisitions, Sony formed Screen Gems with the explicit purpose of producing and distributing low-budget genre films for niche audiences, such as Gary Hardwick's *The Brothers* (2001) and John Carpenter's *Ghost of Mars* (2001). In this respect Sony's two specialist labels would be in a position to compete with Miramax, New Line/Fine Line and Fox Searchlight. Finally, before the end of the decade United Artists – reinvented and relabelled as United Artists Films – became a classics division for MGM, 'crafting a compelling film slate that reflects its proud heritage of nurturing creativity and autonomy' and 'focusing on producing and acquiring eight pics a year, with budgets of less than $20 million'.[33]

The trend continued well into the following decade with Universal, Warner and New Line Cinema establishing their own classics divisions (New Line Cinema terminating Fine Line Features and establishing instead Picturehouse Entertainment in collaboration with cable broadcaster HBO). As is evident, however, the market for 'indie' films had been reshaped drastically by the practices of Disney-backed Miramax and the new classics divisions from the mid-1990s. This was a market that privileged those subsidiaries as, unlike earlier incarnations of classics divisions, these companies did use the conglomerated parents' resources to survive in the market. As an industry analyst put it:

Be it through marketing muscle, superior distribution networks or awards-season campaigns, studio subsidiaries seem to enjoy some distinct advantages – making it even more difficult for smaller companies to release specialty tides [*sic*].[34]

Not surprisingly then, as the transition from independent to 'indie' cinema was taking place in the second half of the 1990s, a considerable number of independent distributors – some with a long and distinguished history in the independent sector, like the Samuel Goldwyn Company – were being driven out of business, leading to further 'indie' market consolidation: Cineplex ODEON folded in 1998; October and Arrow in 2000; Roxie Releasing and Samuel Goldwyn Company in 2001; Trimark in 2002.

These changes started becoming evident only in the next few years and as both labels, 'independent' and 'indie', started being questioned. Back in the mid-to-late 1990s, however, American 'indie' cinema had lived up to its expectations and had fulfilled its promise. In fact it had become so successful and pervasive that in the 1999 Independent Feature Project/West Spirit Awards, James Schamus, independent film writer and producer (with credits in films like *Safe*) and later co-president of Focus Features, argued for the disbandment of the Independent Feature Project (IFP). This was an organisation that was established in 1979, 'on a belief that a truly vital American cinema must include the personal, idiosyncratic, and sometimes controversial voices of filmmakers working outside of the established studio system',[35] and which had grown exponentially in the twenty years since its inception to become a large national association that numbered thousands of members. But, according to Schamus, by 1999 'the IFP ha[d] already, and fabulously, achieved its goals'.[36] And the main goal seems to have been to make independent cinema visible by integrating it successfully into the structures of global production and distribution finance while, importantly, also striving to retain whatever idiosyncrasies (formal, aesthetic, thematic, political, etc.) made such films distinctive in the first place. As Schamus explained:

For all intents and purposes, the films recognized at the Spirits Awards have succeeded overwhelmingly in entering the mainstream system of commercial exploitation and finance, and today the economics required to make oneself heard even as an 'independent' are essentially studio economics. In this so-called independent arena even the 'little guys' need big capital if they are to survive in any economically viable form.[37]

Even though Schamus's view is a far cry from the 1980s independent model, it nevertheless captures clearly the 'indie' model of the mid-to-late 1990s reality: a reality that covers a global 'indie' marketplace, an organised 'indie' industry, a huge 'indie' institutional apparatus and, at the very end of the decade, a remarkably commercially successful 'indie' hit, Artisan's *The Blair Witch Project* (Myrick and Sanchez, 1999), which recorded worldwide cinema box-office takings of $240.5 million, with $140.5 million in the North American market alone.[38] This reality has been sometimes called 'indiewood',[39] a term that clearly brings together the integration between independent cinema and Hollywood that Schamus referred to. That reality represented an extremely important transitional period in the history of the independent sector when a large number of filmmakers with distinctive voices found it easier to finance and produce their often challenging work. David Mamet was one of these filmmakers and *The Spanish Prisoner* is a clear example of 'indie' cinema.

2. David Mamet and 'Indie' Cinema

Introduction

David Mamet is not the first name that springs to mind when thinking about paradigmatic filmmakers from the American independent or 'indie' sectors, and his films have rarely been considered characteristic examples of filmmaking at the margins of Hollywood.[1] As a matter of fact, the whole body of his work in American cinema has attracted very little attention from film scholars and to this date there have been only two book-length studies of his films; one dating back to 1993, when Mamet had made only three films, and one published in 2005, which once again focuses on his early films with only brief discussions of his extensive post-1997 filmography.[2]

Interestingly, both these studies and the majority of critical work on Mamet's cinema have been undertaken by critics located outside the discipline of film studies, and associated more with disciplines like drama and literary studies. This is because Mamet's films constitute a relatively small part of a remarkable artistic output that also includes more than thirty plays, many volumes of collected essays, treatises on cinema and theatre, novels, poetry and a prime-time television show. Not surprisingly then, Mamet's cinema tends to be examined as part of this whole or, as is often the case, in conjunction with his plays, many of which have been adapted for the screen by Mamet himself. Within this particular context, his work has, indeed, attracted very significant and rigorous scholarly attention.

Film critics, on the other hand, have largely stayed away. The main reason behind this oversight is, arguably, what has attracted literature and theatre scholars and critics in the first place, namely that Mamet's cinema is perceived as bound by language, characterised by painstakingly created dialogue that becomes extremely prominent in the same way language becomes prominent in his plays. Writing about *House of Games*, the filmmaker's debut film as a writer-director, Kent Jones acknowledges this emphasis on language clearly:

It was language as fine craftsmanship, every sentence mentally worked and polished by the speaker. It was, as always with Mamet, the sparkling lingua franca of a particular, and particularly tough, moral universe. The rhythms and cadences are recognizably those of their creator, but Mamet offers us more than just a novel verbal flavor. In his plays and films, to speak is not merely to act but to defend one's self.[3]

It was, however, exactly this focus on the undisputed prominence of language in Mamet's films that pushed – unfairly, as I shall argue – questions of visual imagery, *mise en scène* and creativity in the use of film style and construction of narrative to the critical periphery. This was because film critics have traditionally considered cinema a visual medium, while film criticism as an institution has been defined by a long history of privileging the work of filmmakers with a strong visual identity. This tradition has held sway in recent years, as film critics' engagement with 'indie' cinema in the 1990s continued to favour filmmakers with a distinctive visual style, and therefore neglecting filmmakers like Mamet, even though the apparatus of film criticism did flirt with 'less visually arresting' cinema for a short period of time in the 1980s.

Specifically, while the early American independent cinema of the 1980s welcomed issue-driven, dialogue-based films that were tame in terms of aesthetics (such as *Return of the Secaucus Seven* and *My Dinner with André* [Malle, 1981]), the transition to 'indie' cinema of the early 1990s placed particular emphasis on strong visual imagery as a definitive feature of an 'indie' film. This is clearly reiterated in Levy's definition of 'indie' film as 'a fresh, low-budget movie with a gritty style and offbeat subject matter that expresses the filmmaker's personal vision'.[4] Not surprisingly then, critics and the cinema-going public alike identified filmmakers with an eye for overtly visual storytelling as the flag-carriers of American 'indie' cinema. Quentin Tarantino, Steven Soderbergh, Paul Thomas Anderson, Wes Anderson and Richard Linklater, among others, are paradigmatic 'indie' filmmakers who are considered masters in film technique and visual composition and who use their encyclopedic knowledge of world cinema as a vehicle for references to films, filmmakers, styles and art movements.

Unlike such paradigmatic 'indie' filmmakers, however, David Mamet is widely perceived as a filmmaker with no visual flair, a view he helped cultivate himself as in one of his early essays he admitted that he was 'completely ignorant' of the visual aspect of the filmmaking process.[5] This view, in conjunction with the fact that he has enjoyed great success in various other fields ranging from the literary and performing arts to film and theatre criticism and mass entertainment, has led film critics to refuse to take Mamet's filmmaking seriously, especially as most of his films were also box-office failures. For film critics, he is an anomaly, as he has never been a 'full-time filmmaker', while his films, interesting as they might be, tend to be language-driven and therefore weak in visuals. This view was, perhaps, best articulated in an article entitled 'Suspicion' (1998), which was written for leading British film journal *Sight and Sound* by editor-in-chief Nick James. James endorsed this perception of Mamet's cinema unequivocally and explained why Mamet did not deserve the label 'auteur filmmaker', historically a mark of quality for US filmmakers who work within the commercial structures and confines of American cinema, be it mainstream or 'indie'. It is worth quoting this article at some length:

> My own suspicion is that despite the undoubted power and fluency of his writing and the admirable adult complexity and nuance of feeling of his films *House of Games* (1984) [sic], *Homicide* (1991) and *The Spanish Prisoner* (1997), Mamet is not an auteur director. I think this largely because no single image from any of his films is memorable for its own sake. Objects in scenes come readily to mind – the leaking water pistol that exposes the teaser con in *House of Games*; the broken holster that foretells the detective will lose his gun in *Homicide*; the gift book on tennis that places us comfortably in the realm of the ripping yarn in *The Spanish Prisoner* – yet the scenes themselves seem to revel in their visual ordinariness while the dialogue revels in portentousness. Mamet for me remains a playwright who happens to make films, many of which are about mistrusting what you see.[6]

Indeed, David Mamet has been widely considered as one of the most significant and critically acclaimed American playwrights of the twentieth century. Author of landmark plays including *Sexual Perversity in Chicago*, *American Buffalo*, *Glengarry Glen Ross*, *Speed-the-Plow* and *Oleanna*, and recipient of almost every major theatre award (including the prestigious Pulitzer Prize for best American play for *Glengarry Glen Ross* in 1984), he has been canonised in American theatre and has been revered as part of two distinct traditions of 'verbal' playwrights. On the one hand, he has been placed alongside a long tradition of American 'realists', including earlier masters of American drama such as Eugene O'Neill, Tennessee

Williams, Arthur Miller and Edward Albee. On the other hand, he has also been influenced by European 'absurdists' and his name has been often placed alongside those of Samuel Beckett, Harold Pinter and Tom Stoppard. [7]

By 1998, however, the year James's article was published, David Mamet had also been working for seventeen years in American cinema and his output compared favourably with that of any 'full-time' filmmaker who had worked for the same period. By that year, Mamet had written twelve screenplays that were made into theatrical motion pictures, including spectacular commercial and critical successes such as *The Verdict* and *The Untouchables*; five screenplays for made-for-television films, including *A Life in the Theatre* (Mosher, 1993); and five additional screenplays which he directed himself for the cinema: *House of Games* (1987), *Things Change* (1988), *Homicide* (1991), *Oleanna* (1994) and *The Spanish Prisoner* (1997).

Even if, despite all this film work, Mamet would still remain for critics like James predominantly a playwright, his post-1998 career has been almost completely defined by screenwriting and/or directing. He wrote a script that was directed by another filmmaker (*Hannibal* [R. Scott, 2001]); he adapted two of his plays which were directed by other filmmakers (*Lakeboat* [Mantegna, 2000] and *Edmond* [S. Gordon, 2005]); he scripted a made-for-television film (*Lansky* [McNaughton, 1999]); and he wrote four screenplays which he directed for the cinema himself (*The Winslow Boy* [1999], *State and Main* [2000], *Heist* [2001] and *Spartan* [2004]), with a fifth, *Redbelt*, in release at the time of writing. Furthermore, after occasionally writing and/or directing episodes of established television shows like *Hill Street Blues* and *The Shield*, in 2006 Mamet created his own television drama, *The Unit*, which is currently in its third season.

In the same ten-year period (1998–2008), Mamet wrote only three plays, *A Boston Marriage* (1999), *Romance* (2005) and *November* (2008), while also undertaking new adaptations of two existing plays, *Faustus* (2004) and *The Voysey Inheritance* (2005). If nothing else, it is a mistake to continue adopting James's view and instead we should acknowledge that Mamet *is* a filmmaker, *irrespective* of whether he continues to be remarkably prolific in other fields and media. As a filmmaker, he has been closely associated with the American independent and 'indie' sectors.

His first feature as a writer-director, *House of Games*, was produced by Michael Hausman, a leading figure in the early years of the independent cinema of the 1980s with producing credits in *Heartland* (R. Pearce,

1980) and *The Ballad of Gregorio Cortez* (R. Young, 1982). Equally importantly, *House of Games* was financed and distributed by Orion Pictures,
the quintessential independent company of the 1980s which tried to
compete against the studios for most of the decade before being driven
out of business in late 1991.[8] Having built a reputation for being 'a sanctuary for creative filmmakers',[9] and for 'nourishing chancy, low-budget
properties',[10] Orion Pictures must be credited for providing a first-time
filmmaker like Mamet with a particularly attractive environment for
making the transition to film.

Besides exercising minimal creative control (normally in the form of
setting the budget and the schedule for completion) over the production process, Orion was able to fund the film with zero financial risk for
the company, potentially allowing even more creative freedom for the
filmmaker. Around the time of the film's production, in the summer
of 1986, Orion had entered into lucrative agreements and distribution
deals with a number of parties in various media outlets, to the extent that
the company raised the necessary funds to finance all its films for release
in 1986–7. Specifically, by entering into collaborations with HBO (for
cable television), RCA/Columbia (for foreign video) and various foreign
distributors (for cinema releases outside the US), Orion pre-sold its
upcoming films in these ancillary markets, which allowed the company
to continue to operate independently.[11] This enabled Orion to secure
exhibition both in the United States and abroad for a number of offbeat
films such as *Hotel Colonial* (1987), Italian female writer-director's Cinzia
T. Torrini's only American film, and, of course, *House of Games*, a feature
with no established director or marketable stars. With international
distribution and exhibition secure, Mamet found himself in the enviable
position of being able to make his first film according to his – very specific
– vision and hence avoid potential compromises in creative decisions.

In many ways *House of Games* became emblematic of Mamet's cinema,
as the film is characterised by a number of stylistic, narrative and thematic features that would be explored repeatedly in later Mamet films
and which will be discussed in great detail with specific reference to *The
Spanish Prisoner* in Chapters 4 and 5. This chapter, however, would like
to explore the filmmaker's actual position in the American film industry and, especially, the extent to which Mamet's work has been part of
American 'indie' cinema and supported by the very specific institutional
apparatus that emerged around this type of filmmaking. As we shall
see, despite his association with independent cinema from the early

days of *House of Games* in the mid-1980s, for the American film industry he became a recognised 'indie' filmmaker only in the mid-1990s with his fourth feature film, *Oleanna*. It was only then that film distribution companies started advertising his films as 'David Mamet films', and his name started functioning as a marketing hook expected to deliver a specific audience for a specific type of film. In a nutshell, that type of film is always well written, tends to play with various generic frameworks and is permeated by a number of distinct themes, especially deceptive appearances, elusive truths and the shifting nature of reality.

In order to chart Mamet's association with the institutional apparatus of American 'indie' cinema and his development into an auteur within this context, I shall briefly examine the distributors' marketing campaigns for Mamet's films. Specifically, I shall concentrate on the film trailer as a representative sample of an increasingly large number of marketing tools that also include film posters, television and radio spots, publicity stills, press kits, cast and crew interviews, behind-the-scenes and 'making of . . .' documentaries and, more recently, web pages devoted to individual films. As the discussion of the trailers will demonstrate, Mamet the filmmaker became a brand name for the 'indie' sector of the film industry only after the release of *Oleanna* in 1994. From that time to the beginning of the 2000s, Mamet severed his ties with the major Hollywood conglomerates and became strictly associated with the apparatus of 'indie' cinema, which, as we saw in the previous chapter, is primarily exemplified by a huge number of film festivals, specialised cinema circuits, a variety of distribution companies that include independents, major independents and classics divisions, and even an Independent Spirit Award body. Since the early 2000s, Mamet seems to have become a brand name for mainstream Hollywood too, a position I shall address towards the end of this chapter.

American film distribution companies have employed the name 'David Mamet' in five distinct ways when advertising his films, or films he has been involved with as a screenwriter only:

- as a writer making his directorial debut (*House of Games*, 1987);
- through tentative, brief references, which are subordinate to more aggressive forms of star- and genre-based marketing (*House of Games*, 1987; *Homicide*, 1991);
- through an emphasis on his renowned capacity as a genre screenwriter for major motion pictures (*Things Change*, 1988);

- as a critically acclaimed playwright (*Glengarry Glen Ross*, 1992); and
- as a critically acclaimed writer/director (*Oleanna*, 1994; and, in particular, *The Spanish Prisoner*, 1997; *The Winslow Boy*, 1998; *State and Main*, 2000; *Heist*, 2001; and *Spartan*, 2004).

The beginnings of a brand name: David Mamet's films between 1987 and 1993

For *House of Games*, Orion's advertising department orchestrated a marketing campaign that centred on Mamet's transition from a writer to a filmmaker, while also highlighting the film's generic status as a tense noir thriller. The trailer starts with a series of black-and-white stills of sections of the film's US cinema poster, which depicts Lindsay Crouse and Joe Mantegna standing near a large number of signs of pool halls, taverns and card-playing joints. A voice-over runs simultaneously with the stills, revealing that the film constitutes Mamet's entry to filmmaking, while not forgetting to emphasise his talents in writing:

David Mamet. He's got a feel for the way people talk and think and cheat and love; and he's got the Pulitzer Prize to prove it. Now America's most exciting writer makes his directorial debut. Join him in the *House of Games*.

Following this unusual type of prologue, the trailer becomes more conventional as it presents shots from the film. From the very beginning, there is a montage of shots and images that foreground a series of potentially dangerous situations, mostly taking place in dark areas, while upbeat non-diegetic music helps intensify the audience's experience. Very soon, the voice-of-God narrator who appeared in the prologue returns to introduce 'the players' ('a woman of one world seduced by the thrills of another discovering danger in the ultimate high') and the rules of 'the game' the characters/players are seen to be playing. In this manner, the film is pitched as the story of a woman who engages herself in a dangerous game the rules of which she ignores. The trailer finishes with the foregrounding of the names of the film's stars (Lindsey Crouse and Joe Mantegna) in 'David Mamet's *House of Games*', the only instance when the filmmaker's name is mentioned in the main part of the trailer.

What is interesting in Orion's campaign is that the trailer does not make any references to Mamet's previous successful work in Hollywood cinema (Academy Award-nominated screenwriter for *The Verdict*) or his work for the theatre (no reference as to what Mamet received the Pulitzer Prize for). Instead, the distributor emphasises the directorial debut of a celebrated writer and his ability to work within firmly established genre frameworks such as noir and the thriller. This essentially means that Mamet's authorship is more strongly defined by his role as the writer of the film than as its director. This seems to be supported by the fact that the images selected for the *House of Games* trailer suggest that it is a fast-paced, action-packed noir thriller (which, in hindsight, is a totally misleading view). Mamet the director, then, is overshadowed by the writer and therefore becomes a *metteur en scène*, a craftsman, who delivers a conventional genre piece for mass consumption.

Despite the very good reviews, the poor American box office of *House of Games* ($2,585,639) did not prove Mamet's value as a as a marketable commodity in the independent sector, as an auteur brand name who could mobilise specific, niche audiences.[12] However, before the release of his second film (*Things Change*) as a writer-director in October 1988, Mamet found himself attracting considerable attention due to the critical and financial success of Paramount's *The Untouchables*, which he had scripted (and for which he was nominated for a Writers Guild Award for best screenplay based on material from another medium). For this reason, when Columbia Pictures released the trailer for *Things Change* the major tried to capitalise on Mamet's renewed fame as a writer-celebrity, while also following Orion's example in their overall marketing strategy. This means that Columbia marketed the film primarily as a genre piece, in this case a buddy comedy with overtones of gangster elements, aptly summarised in the tagline: 'Bonnie & Clyde . . . Butch & Sundance . . . Gino and Gerry???'.

Like the trailer for *House of Games*, the trailer for *Things Change* also utilises an extra-diegetic narrator, who this time outlines the key generic characteristics of the film when he invites spectators to 'meet two unlikely friends' in an unforgettable weekend at the mafia's expense. After a montage of shots that highlight a Las Vegas iconography, the imagery shifts to comedy by juxtaposing shots of what the protagonists desire (low-profile vacations) with shots of potentially dangerous situations they have dragged themselves into (which attract ample attention). Towards the end of the trailer, the narrator utters: 'From the writer of *The Untouchables* comes a rather unconventional view of unorganised crime', thus employing Mamet's name as a brand name that can guarantee the unfolding of a good (though unconventional) gangster story, targeting the same (large) audience that enjoyed the Elliot Ness versus Al Capone saga in *The Untouchables*. This marketing approach, however, operates to the detriment of Mamet's capacity as the director of the film, since the trailer chooses to ignore that matter completely and closes with a focus on the stars of the film, 'Don Ameche and Joe Mantegna in *Things Change*'. In other words, Mamet's authorship is foregrounded only in terms of story construction and of his proven savvy with the gangster genre and not in terms of his skills as a filmmaker.

After the mixed reviews and the disappointing box-office revenues of *Things Change* ($3,527,886),[13] Mamet concentrated for the following three years on his drama career and returned to filmmaking in 1991 with *Homicide*.[14] The film featured a rather unconventional detective/ conspiracy theory story where the main detective hero (played again by Joe Mantegna) attempts to rediscover his Jewish origins when he is assigned the investigation of a strange murder case of an old Jewish woman, but in the process ends up betraying his colleagues. Mamet's protracted absence from filmmaking, accompanied by the difficult subject matter of the film, led Triumph Releasing Corporation, Columbia's revamped classics division of the early 1980s which distributed the film in the US, to resort to a variety of marketing strategies. These included a strong emphasis on the detective film genre, but mostly on Joe Mantegna, who, during Mamet's break from filmmaking, had established himself as a versatile character actor with credits in Francis Ford Coppola's *The Godfather III* and Woody Allen's *Alice* (both in 1990). The trailer for *Homicide*, therefore, consists of several rapidly edited shots that foreground moments of conflict, whilst an extra-diegetic narrator recites the rather long film tagline: 'Bobby Gold is a cop. A good cop. But, tonight he will betray his friends, disgrace the force, and commit an act of violence because he believes it is the only thing to do.' Accordingly, the trailer closes with the phrase 'Joe Mantegna in David Mamet's *Homicide*', though the emphasis is placed on actor and title rather than the film's director.

The poor box-office receipts (a little less than $3 million) for the third time in Mamet's brief career as a filmmaker point towards the thesis that by 1991 there was a distinct schism in his position in American cinema, which to a degree informed the manner in which his name was used in advertising and publicity for his films and, arguably, also informed the public's lukewarm reception of his work. On the one hand, there was David Mamet the screenwriter, a hot Hollywood property who could deliver distinguished scripts for mainstream genre studio productions accompanied with solid (and occasionally spectacular) box-office results.[15] Conversely, there was David Mamet the marginal writer-director who played with the conventions of different genres (thriller, gangster, buddy movie, conspiracy theory and detective) and opted for medium- or low-calibre stars who under no circumstances could 'open a film'.

The former 'Mamet' had already established a position of power in the American film industry and was well integrated to the structures of the conglomerated Hollywood majors. The latter 'Mamet' (who, arguably, existed due to the success of the former), on the other hand, was relegated to the periphery of Hollywood, working with low budgets and (with the exception of *Things Change*) away from the majors. For this reason, by the early 1990s the name 'David Mamet' could not possibly have signified a concrete reception framework for any of the films he collaborated on. Studio marketing strategies, therefore, dictated the suppression of his celebrity writer status in the critically and financially successful films he scripted, opting to foreground instead the presence of celebrity directors (like Sidney Lumet in *The Verdict*), directors with a distinct visual style (Neil Jordan in *We're No Angels*) or both (Brian De Palma in *The Untouchables*).[16] In contrast, both Columbia Pictures and the independents Orion and Triumph, which marketed the films Mamet scripted and directed, opted for campaigns that were based primarily on the concepts of genre and stars, occasionally championing Mamet's writing skills, while also omitting his credit as a director from the film's promotional material, as in the case of *Things Change*.

Between the release of *Homicide* in October 1991 and his next directorial project, *Oleanna* (November 1994), an adaptation of his own play, Mamet saw his cachet as a filmmaker increasing substantially. This was largely due to another adaptation, this time of his 1984 Pulitzer Prize-winner *Glengarry Glen Ross* for independent distributor New Line Cinema. With a glorious history of record-breaking runs on and off Broadway, *Glengarry Glen Ross* attracted A-list stars (Al Pacino, Alec Baldwin, Ed Harris) as well as several very respectable character actors (Jonathan Pryce, Alan Arkin and a yet to be established Kevin Spacey) and veteran Hollywood star Jack Lemmon, all accepting their parts for drastically reduced salaries. Although Mamet undertook the task of adapting his play for the screen, he did not wish to direct the film. Instead, James Foley was offered the job and almost exactly a year after the release of *Homicide*, *Glengarry Glen Ross* was released, in September 1992. The film's trailer once again suppressed all but one reference to Mamet's authorship, but it turned out to mark a transitory stage in his development as an 'industrial auteur'. This is because the trailer introduced a number of themes that would be picked up by future marketing campaigns for his films as markers of an authorial signature; as distinctly 'Mametian'.

Specifically, following an introductory shot where a group of salesmen are informed that they will lose their jobs if they do not perform to standard, the trailer uses an explanatory intertitle which establishes the story as 'a game' where there can only be one winner. The trailer then divides into two parts separated by the news of a burglary that has taken place in the company's office. In the first part, a rapid editing of shots foregrounds fragments of conversation between the employees, who seem to be planning a burglary of the office they work in, whereas the second part consists of slightly slower edited shots of the aftermath of the burglary, where the same people are accused by the police and accuse each other of the crime. When a policeman's voice is heard asking 'what's your name?', the trailer highlights the film's main assets – its stars – in consequent close-ups: 'Al Pacino, Jack Lemmon, Ed Harris, Alec Baldwin, Alan Arkin in the Pulitzer Prize Winner' (the last phrase is also visible in bold red capital letters), followed by the title of the film in a similar graphic style.

Although Mamet's name is not mentioned in the trailer, he is nevertheless indirectly inferred through the title of the play and the prize he was presented with at the expense of James Foley, the film's director, who remains uncredited. It is obvious that besides the ensemble cast, the real marketing value of the film is the award-winning script, which is represented both visually and aurally at the end of the trailer. More importantly, the trailer for *Glengarry Glen Ross* is also pivotal for establishing Mamet's authorial signature through its themes and motifs, which clearly construct a distinct Mamet(ian) universe. For instance, the 'game' motif, established in *House of Games*, is utilised again in a forceful manner, whereas the theme of betrayal and its consequences (a key concept in the marketing of *Homicide*) is strongly underlined in the fragmented conversations of the characters. For those reasons, the trailer for *Glengarry Glen Ross* pitches the film as an illustrious script with distinct themes served by the talents of superstars and well-respected actors, and directed by a nameless craftsman, who is unwilling (or unable) to make this great script 'his own'.

Despite the good reviews, the star-studded cast and the Pulitzer-winner script, *Glengarry Glen Ross* proved a modest failure, with a gross of

$10,725,228. This failure seemed to support the thesis that Mamet could only be perceived as an industrial commodity as long as he worked within clear-cut genre constraints (film noir [*The Postman Always Rings Twice*], court-room drama [*The Verdict*] and the gangster film [*The Untouchables*]), supported by the performances of stars of the calibre of Jack Nicholson, Paul Newman or Robert De Niro and by the tens of millions of dollars of the major Hollywood studios.

If this was the case, then the decision of the Samuel Goldwyn Company to market his next project, an adaptation of his new Broadway hit *Oleanna*, as an auteur movie, and not as an adaptation, did not make any marketing sense, especially as at the time of the film's release the play was still at the peak of its notoriety and its title carried substantial marketing clout. Ironically, and intriguingly, despite the very limited release and the petty gross of $124,693 (the worst gross for any Mamet film), *Oleanna* established the foundations of Mamet's 'auteur' period, a period in which the filmmaker became associated with the American 'indie' cinema sector. It was after the release of that film that the writer-director emerged as a brand name that could also potentially guarantee a reception framework for a specific audience.

'From the acclaimed writer-director David Mamet': The second period (1994–2001)

Arguably the main difference between the pre- and the post-1994 period in Mamet's position in the American film industry is the filmmaker's 'leave of absence' from the conglomerated Hollywood majors and his smooth integration, this time, into the institutional structures of American 'indie' cinema. For, even when his pre-1994 career seemed to be defined primarily within the independent sector, it was nevertheless always perceived by distributors and film-goers alike as complementary to his better-known career as 'a gun for hire' by the majors. In other words, 'Mamet' as an author-name lacked clear defining characteristics that would eventually attract a desirable (for the distributors of his films) audience, who would automatically respond to every 'David Mamet film'. In this sense it does not seem coincidental that in his second period in his filmmaking career (and until approximately 2001) Mamet did not script another film for a major studio, with the exception of *The Edge* (Tamahori, 1997) for Fox.[17]

The above argument can also be supported by the fact that since *Oleanna* Mamet has been consistently marketed as an 'auteur' for the films he writes and directs, which clearly suggests that the construction of his authorship has become more stable than in the period between 1987 and 1993. This also explains why neither Sony Pictures Classics, distributor of *The Winslow Boy* (1999), nor Fine Line Features, distributor of *State and Main* (2000), felt the need to use Mamet's highly publicised Oscar nomination for best screenplay in 1998 for Barry Levinson's *Wag the Dog* as a marketing hook for promoting their respective films. By the late 1990s, Mamet had become a brand name director who could guarantee a niche audience for distributors of 'indie' films. For this reason, there was no justification for the above-mentioned distributors resorting to old strategies that used his name as a celebrity screenwriter at the expense of his newly established 'indie' filmmaker status. It is now time to examine how this auteur phase has been constructed through a discussion of the trailers for the films he made between 1994 and 2001.

The trailer for *Oleanna* starts with the Samuel Goldwyn Company logo, which gives way to the title 'A Film by David Mamet', thus immediately foregrounding Mamet's name as a guarantor of a specific type of film. The importance of this marketing decision can be stressed by the distributor's refusal to presage the title of the film (by that time the word *Oleanna* was familiar to virtually anyone who had any knowledge of contemporary American theatre) and therefore hook the audience upon the word *Oleanna*. The trailer continues with a relatively fast montage of shots that reveal some information about the plot of the film, emphasising words and phrases uttered by the male character that could potentially carry an ambiguous meaning. Towards the middle of the trailer the first of the two taglines used in the clip appears on the black screen: 'One man, one woman: two truths'. This is followed by a second group of rapidly edited shots that focus, this time, on the female character's point of view (as she accuses her teacher of rape) and on scenes of conflict between the two characters. The clip closes with very large capital letters on a black screen reading: 'DAVID MAMET *OLEANNA*', thus emphasising Mamet's authorship for a second time, and fades to black with the second tagline: 'Whatever side you take . . . You're wrong.'

It is obvious, then, that the Samuel Goldwyn Company's marketing strategy differs considerably from the one advanced by New Line Cinema in *Glengarry Glen Ross* (the other adaptation of Mamet's play in the first half of the 1990s), mainly due to the fact that *Oleanna* did not actually carry the star power of the former. More importantly, the trailer for *Oleanna* does not attempt to sell the film as an adaptation of the play.

In fact, it could be argued that the distributor does not assume that the targeted audience knows the play (there are no references to its huge controversy, nor any reviews by journalists, critics or cultural commentators). Instead, the strategy opted for is a conscious marketing of the film as a David Mamet creation, supported by few references to the subject of sexual harassment in an academic institution. It seems that the distributor attempted to avoid further controversy within a sweeping climate of political correctness in the US, which is why it resorted to a 'tame' marketing technique that did not succeed in generating any awareness of the real nature of the film.

Where the trailer did succeed, nevertheless, was in consolidating Mamet's status as an auteur, since it presented variations of already familiar Mametian themes (deceptive appearances, betrayals, right versus wrong, etc.). It therefore established a pattern of marketing for films written and directed by Mamet that would be invariably employed, improved upon and perfected by Sony Pictures Classics and Fine Line Features, from the mid-1990s to the early 2000s and as his status as a celebrity would steadily increase through his work in several fields of American culture.

An unfortunate exception here was the marketing campaign for yet another adaptation of a Mamet play directed by another filmmaker, *American Buffalo* (Corrente, 1996). The film's distributor, the Samuel Goldwyn Company, did not take into consideration most of the above developments in Mamet's status and devised a trailer that failed to highlight the marketable elements of the film (another famous script, distinct themes associated with Mamet's world), opting instead to concentrate on Dustin Hoffman's performance and on the potential for comedy. Directed by Michael Corrente, who, like James Foley in *Glengarry Glen Ross*, did not receive any credit in the trailer, *American Buffalo* grossed an extremely disappointing $540,364 at the US box-office. The marketing fiasco of *American Buffalo* demonstrated even more forcefully to other distributors that marketing on the basis of Mamet's authorship was an increasingly attractive option. This became particularly evident in the marketing campaign for his next film, *The Spanish Prisoner*. Although I shall examine the marketing of the film in detail in the next chapter, it will be instructive to include here a brief discussion of the trailer that Sony Pictures Classics put in the market to sell the film.

The opening shots are accompanied by three triumphant reviews written in white letters at the bottom of three different frames. These shots consist of fragments of dialogue scenes between various characters, which foreground such themes as trust and betrayal, power and money. When one character utters that he is willing to pay $1,000 for a camera, the screen fades to black and the phrase 'FROM THE ACCLAIMED WRITER AND DIRECTOR DAVID MAMET' appears in large white letters, therefore claiming authorship for the aforementioned themes in the strongest possible way. Masterfully placed towards the beginning of this advertising campaign, the name Mamet functions as an anchor of meaning for the first shots of a trailer that does not have shots of Joe Mantegna, William H. Macy or any other of Mamet's close collaborators who could indirectly suggest his involvement in the picture. Immediately after the authorship credentials, furthermore, there follow a number of shots that reiterate previously established themes and introduce some more (especially the ubiquitous Mamet trademark 'things are not what they appear to be').

Through this marketing strategy Sony Pictures Classics directly invite the viewers to consider the film as a product of David Mamet, aiming at an audience already familiar with his work and the issues that his films tackle. This approach is further supported by other reviews used in the trailer after the naming of the film's stars. In particular, the trailer employs two more reviews, this time both written at the bottom of the frame and repeated by a voice-of-God narrator, 'Mamet's best foray into filmmaking to date' and 'a taut and intriguing tale', which clearly emphasise Mamet's directorial competency and his exceptional storytelling skills, respectively. For all the above reasons, when the title *The Spanish Prisoner* appears on a black screen at the end of the trailer, in exactly the same graphic style as the phrase 'FROM THE ACCLAIMED WRITER AND DIRECTOR DAVID MAMET' earlier, the audience can make no mistake about whom the film was created by.

The critical and commercial success of *The Spanish Prisoner* gave distributors further impetus for marketing Mamet's films on the basis of the filmmaker's name. When he adapted for the screen and directed Terence Rattigan's *The Winslow Boy*, a period costume drama set in Britain, Sony Picture Classics, which took it upon itself to distribute this film too after the success of *The Spanish Prisoner*, resorted to the same marketing strategy even when the film seemed far removed from Mamet's contemporary world of con games, heists and petty criminals. Under the heavy costumes, the make-up and the Edwardian language, however, the film raised questions of deceptive appearances, trust and betrayal, right and wrong; in short, quintessential Mamet themes that had structured all his previous films (and increasingly the trailers that advertised them). For that reason, it is no coincidence that Sony Pictures Classics' promotional clip employed his name with a pomposity not previously seen in trailers for his films.

Like the one for *The Spanish Prisoner*, the trailer for *The Winslow Boy* uses the phrase 'from the acclaimed writer/director David Mamet', this time in extremely large white letters that overwhelm the frame, while at the same time an extra-diegetic narrator reiterates the phrase aurally. Towards the end of the trailer, the title of the film appears against a black background. This time, however, Mamet's name accompanies the title of the film, therefore providing it with a very strong authorial presence – a strategy never before employed for advertising his films. This statement is followed by a few final shots from the film before a third manifestation of his authorship takes place, through the aural affirmation by the extra-diegetic narrator that this is 'the new David Mamet film'.

Although the box-office career of the film in the US was rather disappointing (approximately $4 million gross), bringing into question therefore the effectiveness of such a form of advertising, such a marketing campaign nevertheless makes clear the lengths that film advertising can go to in order to exploit the marketing potential of an auteur brand name, especially when their previous film was critically and commercially successful. As the trailer for *The Winslow Boy* suggests, the name David Mamet carries enough marketing clout to deliver a desirable demographic category for distribution companies such as Sony Picture Classics that, by definition, cater for the more specialised 'indie' film market. It is not surprising, therefore, that Fine Line Features, New Line Cinema's classics division which distributed *State and Main*, followed a similar, though slightly less assured, tactic. Thus, after an emphasis on the comedy elements of the film and in particular on various shots that contain snippets of comic dialogue, yet another extra-diegetic narrator informs the spectator that the trailer advertises *State and Main*, 'a David Mamet film'.

From 'Indie' to Hollywood Auteur: Going Mainstream?

The consistency with which David Mamet's extra-textual authorship has circulated within the context of American 'indie' cinema since the mid-1990s has firmly established the filmmaker as a brand name, despite the modest, and often poor, box-office takings of his films. From this new position of power, in 2001 Mamet attempted to transcend the borders of the institution within which he has been firmly located since *Oleanna* and re-establish his ties with mainstream Hollywood. This is clearly demonstrated in his involvement with MGM and Universal's *Hannibal* and Warner's *Heist*. If his contribution to the extremely successful *Hannibal* might suggest a return to the 'gun for hire' practices of the past, *Heist* signals the filmmaker's first attempt to work with a large budget for a major studio. It would be interesting, for that reason, to examine whether Mamet has now become an industrial auteur for the conglomerated Hollywood majors and what this means for his relationship to 'indie' cinema. The manner in which *Heist*, a multimillion dollar studio-financed thriller, was marketed attests to the fact that Mamet has indeed become a brand name for the majors too, though not to the extent he was during the years of his strict association with 'indie' cinema.

The trailer for *Heist* is characterised by juxtapositions of several blocks of visceral and spectacular shots (car chases, explosions and accidents) that firmly place the film within the fast-paced, action-packed thriller genre, with blocks of dialogue-driven shots that centre on questions of loyalty, betrayal and deceptive appearances and locate the film within Mamet's thematic universe. Like other trailers for his films, the one for *Heist* finishes with a non-diegetic narrator naming the stars of the film and introducing *Heist* as a film 'written and directed by David Mamet'.

Warner's marketing of the film, however, also features a few differences from the marketing practices of the 'indie' distributors. First, the filmmaker's name is used only once, at the end of the text, as against the more prominent use in *The Spanish Prisoner* and *The Winslow Boy*. Second, Mamet's name does not appear on the screen at any point during the trailer apart from the customary final credits shot. Finally, in the juxtaposition of the above blocks of shots, the trailer seems to place more emphasis on generic and spectacular elements at the expense of the more quintessential (for Mamet's films) narrative information and thematic considerations.

On the basis of this evidence, one could argue that the marketing of *Heist* might signal the beginning of a third phase in David Mamet's film career as an industrial auteur, a phase that sees the filmmaker as a relatively solid brand name, who could potentially deliver a large audience for a studio-distributed film. Having previously obtained credentials for such a status from his strict association with American 'indie' cinema, and via his contribution to the enormously successful *Hannibal*, Mamet was 'promoted', though not fully, to an 'industrial auteur proper' within the institutional apparatus of mainstream Hollywood cinema. Unlike 'indie' cinema, however, mainstream cinema is much more susceptible to the size of box-office gross. And yet, despite the fact that *Heist* proved a modest failure in the American box-office,[18] Warner followed a largely similar marketing campaign for *Spartan*, Mamet's penultimate film to date, which, if nothing else, demonstrates the US distributors' belief in the value of authorship as a marketing tool.

Specifically, the trailer combines a series of shots that construct the main narrative enigma (the possibility that white slave traffickers have kidnapped the daughter of a very powerful government official and the deployment of the hero to bring her back) with shots that highlight through dialogue distinctive Mamet themes such as loyalty and betrayal ('we need a man who would follow orders unquestioningly'), and deceptive appearances (the possibility that the government is prepared to let the girl die while on the surface it has mobilised an elaborate plan to find her). These themes are further emphasised by the film's tagline, 'BETRAYAL IS AN ART. COURAGE IS IRRELEVANT. LOYALTY CAN BE DEADLY', which appears in large white letters and interspersed with close-up shots of the four stars of the film, Val Kilmer, Derek Luke, William H. Macy and Ed O'Neill. And unlike the trailer for *Heist*, the trailer for *Spartan* does include a shot where the phrase 'A FILM WRITTEN AND DIRECTED BY DAVID MAMET' appears in a similar graphic style to that of the film's tagline.

The renewed emphasis on the film's director as a marketing strategy, despite the failure of his previous film, is somewhat surprising here and suggests that Warner continues to use Mamet's name to achieve product differentiation for an audience awareness of a film that seems to belong solidly to the suspense thriller genre with no other distinctively marketable elements. One could actually argue that *Spartan* is presented more forcefully than *Heist* as a Mamet film, though again not as compellingly as *The Spanish Prisoner* or *The Winslow Boy*. This reiterates the fact that in this third phase of Mamet's career, the filmmaker has acquired the status of the auteur/brand name that a relatively small number of American directors have been enjoying. This status, however, does not seem to be perfectly secure, as Mamet's authorship is not utilised in the same way or to the same extent as other filmmakers' authorship (such as Scorsese, Tarantino and Woody Allen) and certainly not with the same force as when independent distributors were trying to sell his earlier films.[19]

David Mamet has yet to convince fully mainstream Hollywood that he is the brand name he was during his 'indie' years.' And with *Spartan* recording a major financial failure at the US box-office ($4,373,418) on a same-scale budget as *Heist*, it is debatable whether Mamet's authorship would be used as a selling hook for his films in the near future, or if, indeed, the filmmaker will be 'trusted' again with a big budget and a major production. Perhaps it is a sign that his latest film, *Redbelt*, is an 'indie' production, with Sony Pictures Classics yet again marketing the film in the US market. It is likely this return to the 'indie' sector, as this has been transformed by the third wave of the majors' classics divisions, will mark the beginning of yet a new era in the filmmaker's cinema.

Irrespective of whether Mamet's filmmaking career takes a new turn or whether distributors will still use his name to advertise his future films, his industrial authorship, as it has been constructed by the circulation of his name within specific institutional apparatuses, has signified the existence of a distinctive 'David Mamet film'. As the discussion of trailers demonstrated, a 'David Mamet film' is characterised by several key themes including clashes between right and wrong, betrayals shattering presumed loyalties, a perception of various, often dangerous, situations as games with winners and losers, and all these underlined by a universe where nothing is what it appears to be. Furthermore, a 'David Mamet film' is always expected to be extremely well written and to belong firmly to at least one generic framework, often more than one, and recently with the accompaniment of spectacular elements.

While generally the above description does considerable justice to Mamet's films, this institutionally assigned form of authorship nevertheless has operated to the detriment of an extremely distinctive aesthetic that has characterised all Mamet films and which is primarily the product of the manner in which a very particular use of film style serves an equally distinctly constructed narrative. As I shall argue mainly in Chapter 4, visual style in his films often tends to be counter to dominant ideas of realism and verisimilitude (perceived as defining features of classical filmmaking and mainstream Hollywood cinema) and his stylistic choices tend to convey a different, anti-realist/anti-classical aesthetic. This aesthetic, which is also cultivated by an unusual mode of performance by Mamet's chosen actors is, arguably, more distinctive than his thematics as they were elaborated in this chapter. And yet, this aesthetic has not been highlighted by the distributors' advertising and publicity – though, admittedly, it would be difficult for trailers, posters and television spots to advertise a particular film 'look'.

This argument seems to counter views that consider Mamet's cinema as visually weak and lacking creativity. His film style does not lack visual creativity and it is distinctive in its own way. The difference between Mamet and other celebrated 'indie' filmmakers is that style in his films does not become a vehicle for the articulation of a filmmaker's technical competence or a marker of his or her visual flair, which labels such as 'idiosyncratic' often connote in American 'indie' cinema. Style in Mamet's films exists for purely functional reasons, to support the central 'idea' of his screenplays, and this is nowhere more evident than in *The Spanish Prisoner*.[20]

Before examining how exactly this Mamet aesthetic is created, the following chapter will return to industry and economics and discuss the production history of the film.

3. 'Indie' Film at Work: Producing and Distributing *The Spanish Prisoner*

Introduction

In Chapter 1, I explained how the mid-to-late 1990s became the golden years of 'indie' cinema, an era of opportunity for filmmakers who had not always found it easy to finance their often challenging projects in the preceding years. Fuelled by the incredible commercial success of Miramax, the third wave of classics divisions and the increasing visibility of film festivals like the ultra-hip Sundance, the second half of the 1990s witnessed the increasing integration of a wide variety of films with distinctive characteristics (in terms of aesthetics, political viewpoints, thematic and cultural preoccupations, etc.) into the structures of global production and distribution finance.

This became particularly evident in the period 1995–6, when funding from European investors became readily available for independent films. As a French banker put it in an interview for *Screen International*: '[at that time] demand exceeded supply. We could not make films fast enough. Satellite broadcasters needed product. It did not matter what the film was or who was in it.'[1] And even though this development was very short-lived, it helped make 'indie' films increasingly visible in the international marketplace, especially when the number of crossover commercial hits started growing. Furthermore, and not surprisingly, it also had a major knock-on effect on all film production in the US, which increased exponentially, surpassing the one thousand films per annum mark at the end of the decade, irrespective of the fact that only a fraction of these films ended up finding theatrical distribution.[2]

The Spanish Prisoner was very much a product of this climate. Coming three years after the filmmaker's commercially disappointing but 'auteur-constructing' film *Oleanna*, *The Spanish Prisoner* is exemplified by several central traits that betray its 'indie' roots:

- It was co-produced by independent production companies Jean Doumanian Productions and Sweetland Films, which arranged the financing of the film from sources outside corporate Hollywood.
- It participated in several film festivals, including Toronto and Sundance, in order to secure a cinema distributor.
- It was eventually picked up for distribution following its success at Toronto by Sony Pictures Classics and by a number of local distributors in various territories outside the USA.
- Like other 'indie' films of the time, it featured a cast of actors relatively unknown to the wide public, such as Campbell Scott and Ben Gazzara, alongside Hollywood star Steve Martin, who was cast against type in a small but juicy part.
- It was marketed firmly as an auteur-driven project despite the presence of Martin in the cast, while markers of its 'indie' status were also forcefully utilised by the distributor.
- It enjoyed a limited release in terms of numbers of cinemas in the North American market but also opened in a number of countries outside the US and grossed close to $10 million.
- It was markedly different from major mainstream releases of the time (especially in terms of aesthetics).
- It was received as 'a rarefied taste' by the popular press.[3] Interestingly, though, while most film reviews attributed the film's distinctiveness to the filmmaker, they did not approach the film as an example of 'indie' cinema.

The next two chapters will deal with the film's distinctive aesthetics in detail. This chapter will discuss the film's production and distribution history.

Production

The film's production history started with Mamet approaching independent film and theatre producer Jean Doumanian with his script for the film in 1995. At that time, Doumanian, who started her career in television as one of the producers of *Saturday Night Live* in the 1980s, had started making a name for herself in the film industry when she became the producer of Woody Allen films, starting with *Bullets over Broadway* (1994) and *Mighty Aphrodite* (1995). Prior to his collaboration with Doumanian, Allen had enjoyed a long-standing production and distribution relationship (from the mid-1970s to 1990) with United Artists and Orion Pictures and had ended up at Columbia/TriStar following ex-United Artists and Orion executive Mike Medavoy, who became the head of TriStar in 1991. Doumanian, however, convinced Allen to leave TriStar after only two pictures and offered him a production deal that gave him not only complete creative control but increased funding for his films and better financial terms for himself.

According to the deal, Allen's films would be produced through Sweetland Films, a company that Doumanian had originally established in 1991 to produce Sven Nykvist's film *Oxen* [*The Ox*] and which eventually became a 'European-backed financing vehicle for Doumanian's [film] projects'.[4] With Allen's film's enjoying considerable commercial success in Europe, despite the filmmaker's decline of popularity in the US, Doumanian managed to secure 'a multimillion-dollar line of funding'[5] which would also extend for films made by filmmakers other than Allen. With *Bullets over Broadway* and *Mighty Aphrodite* proving both commercial and critical hits, Doumanian decided to look at other potential projects for the 'Sweetland package'.

In February 1995 Doumanian produced for the stage *Death Defying Acts*, three one-act plays written by Mamet, film writer and director Elaine May and Woody Allen, put together in one show. It was during the Broadway production of *Death Defying Acts* that Mamet approached Doumanian with the script for *The Spanish Prisoner*, which was based on an unpublished play he had written several years earlier. With Mamet's reputation as a filmmaker growing, especially as he had started becoming firmly associated with the independent sector, it became clear to Doumanian that *The Spanish Prisoner* was an excellent project to finance with the Sweetland funds. Doumanian assumed the role of the film's producer, with J.E Baucaire and Letty Aronson, Woody Allen's sister, holding executive producer roles as Sweetland Films' principals. The producing package became complete when Sarah Green, producer of other films associated with Mamet (*Oleanna* and *American Buffalo*), and strongly linked with independent cinema through her long-term professional relationship with John Sayles (she had produced *City of Hope* [1991], *Passion Fish* [1992] and *The Secret of Roan Inish* [1995]), became attached to the project as a co-producer.

With finance secure and production arrangements complete, Mamet proceeded to cast the film. Although in his previous four films he had used a group of actors who had been associated with him for a number of years through his work in the American theatre, including Joe Mantegna, Mike Nussbaum and William H. Macy, for *The Spanish Prisoner*, Mamet gave three of the main parts of the film to actors outside his 'stage circle'. These included iconic character actor Ben Gazzara, who has been strongly associated with American independent cinema through his collaboration in a number of films with John Cassavetes, arguably the most influential figure in the independent sector; Campbell Scott, an actor with many credits in small 'indie' films, including *The Daytrippers* (Mottola, 1996) and *Big Night* (Tucci and Scott, 1996), the latter a film that Scott co-wrote and co-directed; and finally Hollywood comedian Steve Martin, who was cast against type as the playboy-turned-con man, Julian Dell. Although Martin seemed a surprise choice for a Mamet film, the filmmaker considered Martin right for such a dramatic role after he had seen the star performing alongside Robin Williams in a production of Samuel Beckett's *Waiting for Godot* in 1988.[6] The smaller parts in the film, however, were still entrusted to actors familiar with Mamet's work, such as Felicity Huffman, Ricky Jay and Rebecca Pidgeon. This idiosyncratic mix of actors gave the film a slightly different air from other Mamet productions that utilised only actors who have been professionally trained by him. It also made the film a more commercial proposition, given Martin's star status and Gazzara's and Scott's plethora of previous credits.

As a relatively small 'indie' production, the film's budget did not surpass the $10-million-dollar mark, while the shoot was completed in just 36 days.[7] Mamet's pragmatic approach to filmmaking, which has always involved a detailed organisation of the shoot during preproduction,[8] in tandem with the actors' good understanding of the lighting of the film, which kept the number of takes and camera set-ups to a bare minimum, helped the film come in on budget and on schedule.[9] Upon its completion, Doumanian made the decision to send the film to a small number of festivals and attract the attention of distributors in this way, rather than screening the film for individual distributors without having first tested the audience's reactions or checked the response of the press. This particular approach to securing distribution was opted for mainly because, while at the Cannes Festival in May 1997, Doumanian had succeeded in selling distribution rights of Allen's upcoming film *Deconstructing Harry* as well as a documentary about his jazz-band tour entitled *Wild Man Blues* (Kopple) to Fine Line Features for a very attractive price.[10] Doumanian believed that she could achieve the same for Mamet's film, given its several attractive selling points.

Acquisition for Distribution

The film premiered at the Toronto International Film Festival in September 1997. Prior to its screening the film had generated significant buzz and was deemed one of the most 'highly anticipated' films of the festival, alongside other eagerly expected 'indies' such as *The Apostle* (Duvall, 1997), *Henry Fool* (Hartley, 1997) and *Boogie Nights* (P. T. Anderson, 1997). For that reason *The Spanish Prisoner* was awarded 'Special Presentation' status and was allocated a prime slot in the festival schedule, which naturally enhanced further its public visibility.[11] According to a *Variety* festival report, the film (alongside *The Apostle*, *Henry Fool* and a few others) was one of the top targets for independent distributors and classics divisions that have routinely frequented Toronto and a few other key festivals looking for completed films with a view to buying their distribution rights.[12]

True to expectations, the film generated very positive responses from the audience, attracting the attention of six distributors specialising in the 'indie' film market, including established classics division Sony Pictures Classics and large independent Trimark Pictures. After a bidding war, Sony Pictures Classics secured distribution rights for the North American cinema and home video markets,[13] while a number of established foreign distributors with expertise in the arthouse film market purchased the film's rights for numerous territories outside the US: Bac Films Distribution for France; Pathé Image for the UK, Cecchi Gori Group for Italy and Kinowelt Filmverleih for Germany.

Following the film's acquisition for cinema distribution in the US, Mamet, Doumanian and Sony Pictures Classics decided to build further on word-of-mouth for the film by delaying its release for a few months and by submitting the film to a number of key festivals, hoping for further exposure to arthouse/'indie' audiences and press. They also hoped to benefit from positive word-of-mouth coming from Europe (especially France), where the film enjoyed an early release. In terms of film festivals, naturally, Sundance was at the top of the list and *The Spanish Prisoner* was submitted for the 'Premieres' programme of the festival, for which it was selected alongside a number of other films that became 'indie' hits in the same year as Mamet's film, including: *Affliction* (Schrader, 1997), *The Opposite of Sex* (Roos, 1998) and *The Real Blonde* (Di Cillo, 1997).

With the Sundance stamp on it, the film also went to the Rotterdam International Film Festival in February 1998, the Miami Film Festival in the same month and the Cleveland International Film Festival in March.[14]

By that time, six months after its world premiere in Toronto, the film was ready for commercial distribution in the US, especially as the reviews of the film following its release in Europe were also very positive. Before examining the manner in which the film was marketed and released in the US, however, it is important to provide a brief history of the film's US distributor, Sony Pictures Classics, as, in its various incarnations, it has been a leading force in the independent and 'indie' sectors and because the film's success is indeed intricately linked with the company's chosen marketing strategy and, generally, its savvy in the arthouse/'indie' market.

The Sony Pictures Classics Factor

Sony Pictures Classics is nothing short of a phenomenon in the American film industry. Although the company was formally established on 1 January 1992, its management team of Tom Bernard and Michael Barker (who co-chair the company) had been in place since 1980, when together they headed United Artists Classics, the first ever contemporary classics division. While there, Bernard and Barker, together with Donna Giglioti, established the rules of the arthouse film market as it was shaped in the 1980s. These included:

- selection of a small number of non-US films each year, especially ones made by reputable auteurs;
- securing their North American cinema and home video distribution rights;
- building a marketing campaign that centres on the filmmakers and/ or the cultural capital of the film, which is treated as a 'piece of art';
- releasing the film slowly and carefully without great advertising expenditure; and
- targeting primarily the arthouse film audience, a substantial part of which exists in major metropolitan areas such as New York, Los Angeles and San Francisco.

Modeling their business on a distribution system that was originally developed by United Artists in the 1960s through their Lopert Pictures subsidiary, United Artists Classics simply updated the system for the 1980s, especially as the company worked under the tutelage of the same people who had brought Lopert to United Artists in the 1960s (Arthur

Krim, Robert Benjamin and Eric Pleskow). As Lopert had brought to specialised American theatres in the 1960s such European classics as *Never on Sunday* (Dassin, 1960), *La Notte* [*The Night*] (Antonioni, 1962) and *Persona* (Bergman, 1967), United Artists Classics reignited interest in the arthouse film with the release of modern classics of world cinema such as *Lili Marleen* (Fassbinder, 1981), *La Dernier Metro* [*The Last Metro*] (Truffaut, 1980) and *Diva* (Beineix, 1981) – with the last two proving substantial successes at the US box-office.[15]

When Krim and Benjamin left United Artists and formed Orion Pictures they quickly established a new classics division in 1983, Orion Classics, and invited the United Artists Classics team to head it. For the rest of the decade, Orion Classics dominated the arthouse film market, releasing some of the most widely acclaimed non-US films, including *Ran* (Kurosawa, 1985), *Himmel Über Berlin* [*The Wings of Desire*] (Wenders, 1987) and many Pedro Almodovar films, including the extremely financially successful *Mujeres al borde de un ataque de nervios* [*Women on the Verge of a Nervous Breakdown*] (1988). By that time, the majors that had rushed to follow United Artists' example and set up their own classics divisions (Universal Classics, 20th Century Fox International Classics) realised that the arthouse market required a very specialised knowledge of world cinema, while it could also not support a large number of distributors. One by one the first wave of the classics divisions folded, including United Artists Classics, which stopped trading early in 1984, only a few months after its management team had left to head Orion Classics. In this respect, Orion Classics operated largely unopposed, with some small independent distributors like Cinecom and Island assuming the form of competition.

While dominating the non-US arthouse film market, Orion Classics gradually also started acquiring the distribution rights of low-budget, independently produced American films such as *Strangers Kiss* (Chapman, 1983) and *Old Enough* (Silver, 1984), and later in the 1980s and in the early 1990s released influential independent films like *Mystery Train* and *Slacker*. However, the financial problems of its parent company, Orion Pictures, which eventually was driven out of business in 1991, put an end to the division. For Barker, Bernard and Marcie Bloom (who had replaced Giglioti in 1989), though, the end of Orion Classics signalled the beginning of yet another classics division. Days after the collapse of the company they were offered the reins of Sony's (Columbia's) vehicle for securing a slice of the non-US arthouse/US independent film market, Sony Pictures Classics.

The key to understanding Sony Pictures Classics and its prior incarnations can be found in four unassailable principles that characterised
the company:

- autonomy from the operations of the parent company;
- small-scale operations;
- management stability; and
- adherence to distribution policies that are 'labour intensive rather
  than capital intensive'.[16]

Having established the rules in arthouse film distribution while in United
Artists Classics, and developed a track-record that has been unparal-
leled 'in terms of continuity and profitability', the division's management team has always been allowed to 'operate with a unique degree of
autonomy'.[17] This has been so to such an extent that the division is often
perceived as independent from corporate Hollywood.[18]

The unique degree of autonomy with which Sony Pictures Classics
has operated within the corporate structure of a Hollywood major is
in many ways a product of its management's success while at Orion.
Having built a good relationship with the heads of Orion while all parties
were still at United Artists, the management of Orion Pictures stood
away from interfering with the decisions and distribution practices the
classics division adopted, allowing them the freedom to create a subsidiary with a distinct identity.[19] In return, Orion Classics maintained profitability throughout the years, which, remarkably, has also been the case
throughout the history of Sony Pictures Classics,[20] despite the changes in
the distribution game that took place with the introduction of the third
wave of classics divisions in the mid-1990s.

Although the entry into the market of companies like Fox Searchlight,
Paramount Classics and Focus Features, which, alongside the tremen-
dously successful Miramax in the 1990s, drove film acquisition rights'
costs and advertising and publicity expenditure sky-high, Sony Pictures
Classics remained persistently a small-scale operation, refusing to adopt
several of the practices that characterised the third wave of classics divisions. Thus, while classics like Fox Searchlight often pool the parent company's resources to release their films nationwide (see Chapter 1), Sony
Pictures Classics has stuck to its platform release approaches, pooling
Sony's vast resources only on the rare occasion when a film shows that it
has the potential to become a breakaway success. This happened in 2001

with the astounding success of *Wo hu cang long* [*Crouching Tiger, Hidden Dragon*] (Ang Lee, 2000), which eventually grossed $128 million, but which first spent five weeks on limited release before going nationwide with the parent company's help.

Equally, while companies like Focus Features are 'allowed' to produce films with budgets of up to $30 million but subject to the parent company's approval,[21] which, not surprisingly, comes with 'a mandate to make mainstream movies that make money',[22] Sony Pictures Classics' business strategy has remained 'distribution volume' (releasing a number of films with potentially all of them securing a small profit rather than going for the big hit, the grosses of which will offset the losses of many others). Even in the 2000s, when distribution costs have reached levels that have prompted the trade press to pronounce that 'little profits are not enough these days' for classics divisions,[23] Sony Pictures Classics has remained the exception, continuing its emphasis on volume with almost 20 releases in 2007 and 2008, demonstrating the consistent benefits of its fiscally conservative approach to distribution.

At the core of the Sony Pictures Classics approach has been a masterful use of the platform or limited release model of distribution. According to this model, a film opens only in a limited number of cinemas – often fewer than ten screens – in major metropolitan areas like New York, Los Angeles and Chicago, which are known for their strong arthouse/'indie' cinema culture. A platform release allows a film to establish itself in the marketplace and slowly build positive word-of-mouth that should eventually attract more viewers without the distributor bearing any additional advertising expenditure (especially ultra-expensive television advertising). If the film proves successful and word-of-mouth brings viewers consistently in the limited number of screens, then the distributor expands it and invests accordingly in further advertising.

As is obvious, this model of distribution suits small, less well-capitalised distributors that cannot afford to spend millions in advertising for films that might not prove commercial hits. Platform release has often proved ultra-successful, however, especially in relation to specific auteur-driven films that for any aesthetic, political and/or thematic reasons could have found it difficult to attract a significant audience in a straight nationwide release. Even major Oscar-winning hits like *Platoon* (Stone, 1986) and *Dances with Wolves* (Costner, 1990) were platformed on limited release to build word-of-mouth before expanding nationwide and finding astounding commercial success.[24]

Sony Pictures Classics demonstrated its skills in platform releasing from the very first year of its operation with the success of British film *Howards End* (Ivory, 1992), which was kept in the box-office charts for more than a year on limited release, finally grossing $26 million and becoming a major commercial hit.[25] Although this level of commercial success was a rare occurrence for the sector in the early 1990s, the company's early films enjoyed remarkable critical success, which was often translated into solid box-office results. Specifically, Sony Pictures Classics' films were awarded the Oscar for Best Picture in a Foreign Language three years in a row, starting with *Indochine* (Wargnier, 1992) and then *Belle Epoque* (Trueba, 1993) and *Utomlyonnye solntsem* [*Burnt by the Sun*] (Mikhalkov, 1994). By 1995 the company had fully stabilised its operations and had become a force in the market, with a charter to 'acquire, market and distribute 9 to 14 films a year, each budgeted btw $100,000 to $5 million'.[26]

Despite developing a deserved reputation for being an expert in distributing non-US films, in the words of its management, Sony Pictures Classics' 'major bread and butter' has been American films.[27] Prior to *The Spanish Prisoner*, the company had distributed, mostly successfully, some of the most famous 'indie' titles, including *Orlando* (Potter, 1993), *Mi vida loca, Living in Oblivion* (Di Cillo, 1995), *Safe, Amateur, Lone Star, Welcome to the Dollhouse* (Solondz, 1996), *SubUrbia*, and *In the Company of Men* (La Bute, 1997). In this respect, its acquisition of *The Spanish Prisoner* meant that the company had perceived the film as an arthouse/'indie' production that had to establish itself first with the art cinema audience before potentially expanding it to more screens and targeting larger audiences. In Sony Pictures Classics, Doumanian and Mamet found a savvy distributor that could potentially make *The Spanish Prisoner* the first of Mamet's films to find a large audience and succeed commercially.

Distribution

After building considerable word-of-mouth by screening the film in important festivals, Sony Pictures Classics finally opened the film in an almost exclusive release (just seven screens) on 4 April 1998. With Mamet's film characterised by a distinctive aesthetic that had the potential to alienate a large audience, despite its strong generic status, the company believed that an exclusive release would give the film the necessary time to assert itself in the marketplace. Helped by the buzz that had been built in the previous months and by the – hopefully – positive reviews from the US press, Sony Pictures Classics had confidence that *The Spanish Prisoner* would win the arthouse/'indie' audience.

The second and more important reason behind the distributor's choice to open *The Spanish Prisoner* in this manner was that the film's two main selling points (Martin's star persona and Mamet's author-ship) were sufficient to attract a significant portion of the arthouse audience but arguably not enough to target large mainstream audi-ences and to compete with major films. Although Mamet's reputa-tion in American cinema had been consolidating after ten years as a writer-director, as I argued in Chapter 2, he was still unknown as a filmmaker to the large cinema-going public. Martin, on the other hand, was a major Hollywood star with a body of comic performances that were based on his physical, often acrobatic, skills. His role in *The Spanish Prisoner*, however, was not a comic one, making questionable a marketing campaign that would revolve around his presence in the film. Yet, if his against-type performance was 'accepted' by the film's first viewers and the press, then Sony Pictures Classics would have a major marketing tool in its hands with which to tap into the vast mainstream audience.

Given these issues, and after deciding to release the film in platform and gradually increase its playdates by exploiting good reviews and positive word-of-mouth, Sony Pictures Classics' marketing campaign highlighted four main points:

- authorship;
- achievement;
- 'indie' status; and
- narrative and genre.

In a nutshell, Sony Pictures Classics tried to sell *The Spanish Prisoner* as 'a David Mamet film' that represents, according to critics, his finest hour in terms of cinematic achievement; deals with elaborate confidence games and deceptive appearances; and is a product of the 'indie' sector. In this respect, the company targeted mainly Mamet's fans and arthouse/'indie' audiences while also highlighting the film as a genre movie in the hope of attracting some mainstream audiences. This approach was evident in the film's trailer, which I discussed briefly in the previous chapter and aspects of which I would like to highlight here too.

From the opening shot of the trailer, the distributor underscores the film's 'indie' status by citing famous *New York Times* film critic Janet Maslin's description of it, 'the unequivocal hit of the Sundance Film Festival', as well as the film's kinship with successful, well-known films that feature elaborate plots, like *The Usual Suspects* and *North by Northwest*. Sony Pictures Classics then quotes well-known *Los Angeles Times* critic Kenneth Turan, who highlights both achievement and narrative complexity (the latter also a key characteristic of the con game genre, as I shall discuss in Chapter 5) in his phrase 'an elegant puzzler'.[28] Only then does the trailer move to anchor all those reviews and fragments from the film that appear in the trailer with the phrase 'FROM THE ACCLAIMED WRITER AND DIRECTOR DAVID MAMET'.

Following this, the trailer presents the film's stars in successive shots and with an extra-diegetic narrator reciting each individual's name. Interestingly, however, Steve Martin is not presented first (or last) in a potential effort to highlight his presence in the film. Instead, he is presented third, after Campbell Scott and Rebecca Pidgeon, who have more screen time than him in the film. In this respect, Martin's stardom is contained, as the trailer does not want to attract special attention to his presence in case potential audiences get the wrong idea about the film. In subsequent shots, the trailer revisits three of the four focal points of the campaign (skipping the 'indie' status element) through two more reviews, which, this time, are not only written on the screen (like the previous three) but also heard from the voice of the extra-diegetic narrator:

- Critics call it 'David Mamet's best ever foray into filmmaking' (*Details Magazine*)
- A taut, intriguing tale (Marie Caro, *Chicago Tribune*)

For all the above reasons, when the title *THE SPANISH PRISONER* appears on a black screen at the end of the trailer, in exactly the same graphic style as the phrase 'FROM THE ACCLAIMED WRITER AND DIRECTOR DAVID MAMET' appeared in earlier, it is obvious that the distributor aimed primarily for the arthouse/ 'indie' audience that are familiar with Mamet's work before specifically targeting any other audiences.

A similar approach is evident in the poster produced to promote the film, the image of which has been chosen as the cover for this book.[29] The poster features Campbell Scott and Rebecca Pidgeon, in character, in a social encounter that could suggest the possibility of romance. Where the emphasis seems to lie, though, is on Scott removing his sunglasses (or putting them on?), arguably suggesting that the encounter (and the whole film) is about his (lack of) vision, what he can or cannot see, and the fact that appearances are deceptive, the quintessential theme in Mamet's cinema and in *The Spanish Prisoner* in particular. Furthermore, as I shall argue in Chapter 5, the failure of cognitive skills in general and vision in particular (both in terms of a character's relationship to other characters and in terms of the spectator's perception of narrative events) is at the core of the con game film genre, a characteristic example of which is *The Spanish Prisoner*.

Besides nodding to narrative and genre, the poster brings together the main aspects of the campaign through yet more use of reviews, while the names of the stars of the film are afforded some space too. As in the trailer, Janet Maslin is invoked again in white large capital letters that contrast well with the black background of the poster:

THE MOST UNEQUIVOCAL HIT OF THE SUNDANCE FILM FESTIVAL. THE MOST SATISFYING FEAT OF GAMEMANSHIP MR MAMET HAS YET BROUGHT TO THE SCREEN.

Furthermore, again as in the trailer, Martin's name is not afforded special status, as the actors' names appear this time in alphabetical order. What is actually given more status and visibility is the director's name, and the poster makes yet another strong use of authorship by including, under the title of the film, the phrase 'A DAVID MAMET FILM'.

Finally, Sony Pictures Classics chose two taglines to represent the film further in its advertising, both of them directly referring to the film's generic status as a con artist/con game film:

- It's the oldest con in the book.
- Can you really trust anyone?

By associating the filmmaker with a particular genre (proclaiming, moreover, that the filmmaker in question is the 'master' of the genre at the peak of his career), the marketing of *The Spanish Prisoner* also tried to build a distinct identity for a film that, as trade publications predicted, could prove to be 'a tough sell', but which 'critical support withstanding, could post impressive numbers in limited release'.[30]

Release and Box Office

The film's exclusive opening on seven screens on 4 April was accompanied by extremely promising results.[31] Taking on average $17,716 per screen, *The Spanish Prisoner* recorded by far the best average per screen of all films on release in that particular week, second only to *Everest* (a film made for the IMAX cinemas). As highly anticipated films on limited release tend to produce box-office results like this in their opening weekend, however, a film cannot be dubbed a success unless these results remain correspondingly high in the following week (or even weeks) as the film gradually tries to assert itself in the marketplace by opening in more screens.

Almost tripling its playdates in its second week (eighteen cinemas), *The Spanish Prisoner* achieved similar results then, taking $12,503 per engagement, and the same story was repeated in its third week of release, managing $10,215 from thirty-one screens. This suggests that the film had generated substantial and, more importantly, sustained interest in arthouse/'indie' audiences, providing the foundation for Sony Pictures Classics to move to a more aggressive, though always limited, release.[32]

In the following four weeks, then, the distributor took the film to 126, 178, 296 and 340 engagements, respectively (with the last also representing the peak of the film in terms of cinema numbers), in order to capitalise on its promising start. Despite an expected drop in per-cinema average, the film's weekend box office remained steady, averaging over $800,000 in box-office gross in each of the four weekends in question, and totalling $4,804,408 during its peak weak, already surpassing the box-office gross of every other Mamet-directed film.

Having reached a peak point in the seventh weekend, Sony Pictures Classics then started gradually to decrease the number of screens on which *The Spanish Prisoner* played. In this respect it maintained relatively strong results as the film continued to attract viewers, especially in New York and Los Angeles, where the film continued posting strong figures.[33] For the following five weeks (weeks 8–12 of its release), the film continued playing on over 100 screens, and almost doubled its total gross for the North American market to $8,329,451 by the end of its twelfth week of release. The film continued playing for sixteen more weeks in an average of fifty cinemas per week, finally ending its run in the first week of November 1998, half a year after its opening and with a final gross of $9,582,900.

Although the figure seems relatively small given the film's commercial elements, and especially its costs, with the budget alone standing at $10 million, it is imperative to put these figures in their right context. In his review of the summer film season for 1998, *Variety* critic Leonard Klady names *The Spanish Prisoner* as one of the key films in 'a potent season' for the 'specialized sector', which managed to record 'hefty grosses of between $5 million and $10 million' alongside similar films such as *The Opposite of Sex* and *Smoke Signals* (Eyre, 1998).[34] After all, these were still the years before *The Blair Witch Project* revolutionised both film marketing and the level of box-office grosses 'indie' films could reach. These were still the years when crossover hits were on the increase but the $10-million mark was a difficult hurdle to get over, unless the films broke out nationwide. As it happened, for 1998 *The Spanish Prisoner* was 'the highest-grossing specialized film of the year';[35] and this in a year that also saw the release of other well-known 'indies', including ones with equal or greater commercial potential and star power than Mamet's film (*Gods and Monsters* [Condon] and *Your Friends and Neighbors* [La Bute]), as well as critical successes (*Velvet Goldmine* [Haynes], *High Art* [Cholodenko], *Happiness* [Solondz], *Pi* [Aronofsky] and *Men with Guns* [Sayles]). In this respect, *The Spanish Prisoner* should be seen as a modest failure only because it did not manage to recoup its negative costs and not because it did not gross more dollars at the US box office.

For Sony Pictures Classics, however, the film was an unmitigated success. It grossed more than any other of its films in that particular year and contributed greatly to a record financial year for the company.[36] Furthermore, alongside *Afterglow* (Rudolph, 1997), another film Sony Pictures Classics distributed in 1998, *The Spanish Prisoner* became the first in the company's history to play on such a large number of screens, foreshadowing the company's spectacular success in the following years with the wide distribution of runaway hit *Crouching Tiger, Hidden Dragon*. As a final marker of the film's success for the company, Sony Pictures Classics proceeded to pre-buy the distribution rights for the following Mamet film, in effect financing the $5-million production of *The Winslow Boy*.

Conclusion

Although rarely invoked, *The Spanish Prisoner* remains a quintessential example of an 'indie' film during a remarkable time for the sector. With finance provided by an independent company that exploited the then abundance of production capital outside the US, and with the actual production process of the film headed by two producers with considerable expertise in the sector, the road was wide open for a filmmaker with a distinctive aesthetic vision, like David Mamet, to create a film without having to compromise his filmmaking practice. On the other hand, specialty label Sony Pictures Classics distributed the film with great savvy, turning it into the most commercially successful Mamet film. Chapter 4 will highlight the features of Mamet's distinctive practice and discuss the 'anti-classical' aesthetics of his filmmaking as this is evident in *The Spanish Prisoner*.

4. 'That's what you just think you saw!' Narrative and Film Style in *The Spanish Prisoner*

Everything that happens in *The Spanish Prisoner* is a trick. Every character, even the hobbling old lady you think is just a dress extra, is present for a purpose. Every remark, however apparently trivial, merits careful examination.[1]

Introduction: Deceptive Appearances and Elusive Truths

If there is a theme that appears in all Mamet films and often tends to dominate and overwhelm other distinctive themes that permeate his body of work in American cinema, that theme is 'deceptive appearances' and the tendency of people to misinterpret reality, often with dire consequences. Potentially every sequence, scene or even shot in a Mamet film can function as a smokescreen, hiding underneath a completely different layer of reality. And even when this deeper layer of reality is revealed underneath the surface, it is quite often the case that this is yet another smokescreen with reality and truth buried even deeper, to the extent that it becomes questionable whether reality is indeed accessible for characters and spectators alike. A good example of this is the scene discussed in the opening pages of this book. Joe Ross and Susan Ricci's verbal interaction on the plane to New York was originally perceived as Joe's attempt to 'entertain' himself by cultivating in Susan's mind the possibility of romance with him, only for this to turn out to be a precisely calculated move by Susan as part of her role in an elaborate confidence game designed to make Joe hand in his ultra-precious invention.

This constitutive element of Mamet's work is even present in the very first scene of *The Spanish Prisoner*. Prior to their flight to the Caribbean and while at the airport, George Lang had asked a sales assistant to show him some expensive cigars. The assistant, who appeared only briefly in one shot of the scene, handed Lang the cigars and the scene then moved to a different direction. Several scenes later, the multimillionaire Jimmy Dell arrived on the island of St Estephe with his mistress, a princess married to one of his friends. Neither Joe nor the spectator gets to see the princess's face. Towards the end of the film, however, when protagonist and spectator alike begin to realise that a swindle has been under way, the film's narration reveals the sales assistant and the princess to be the same person, who simply filled in two different parts in the confidence game.

One could even go as far as to argue, as Temenuga Trifonova has done, that the confidence game that structures the plot in *The Spanish Prisoner* is in actual fact two distinct, elaborate confidence games that take place at the same time: on the one hand, there is a fake but evident swindle, one that makes Joe think that people around him are trying to con him. On the other hand, there is a real but latent scam, one which is taking place at exactly the same time as Joe is trying to defend himself from the fake one, and which he cannot see.[2] According to Trifonova, the structure of a confidence game within a confidence game creates the proposition – a complicated one for the spectator – that Joe needs to believe that he is being tricked (fake con, what happens in the surface and what the spectator sees) in order for the con artists to execute their plans (real con, what happens in reality and what the spectator does not see). In Trifonova's own words:

[In *The Spanish Prisoner*] the real is the result of the unreal flaunting its unreality: attaining self-awareness the unreal becomes real, just as a lie, by drawing attention to itself, passes for truth. The real remains suspect, nevertheless, since the unreal is not supposed to 'know' that it is unreal.[3]

This remarkable open-endedness, which is largely created by the existence of layers of deceptive appearances and elusive truths in Mamet's films and is especially emphasised in his films about con artists and their scams, like *The Spanish Prisoner*, suggests that the narratives of his films might not adhere to the rules of mainstream classical Hollywood cinema. This means that they might break away from strongly established conventions such as causality, psychological character motivation and continuity, and might not follow the principles of unity and clarity that normally help create airtight narratives where all pieces of the story come neatly together at the end of the film. As Kristin Thompson has suggested in her influential study of contemporary American cinema, *Storytelling in the New Hollywood: Understanding Classical Narrative Technique*:

The most basic principle of the Hollywood cinema is that a narrative should consist of a chain of causes and effects that is easy for the spectator to follow. This clarity of comprehension is basic to all our other responses to films, particularly emotional ones.[4]

Instead, narrative in Mamet's films, and especially in *The Spanish Prisoner*, tends generally to follow the above conventions, but, significantly, on many occasions it also departs from these rules and principles. These departures mainly take the form of narrative events that fail to find motivation or justification in the story; characters' decisions that are difficult, often impossible, to explain; a number of coincidences that stretch considerably the suspension of the spectators' disbelief; and a mode of dialogue delivery that often differs so drastically from dialogue delivery in the average Hollywood film that it makes the characters in Mamet's films simply not believable. These departures affect significantly the extent in his films of narrative clarity and unity, which, again according to Thompson:

demand that everything in the film should be motivated, whether in advance or in retrospect; that is each event, object, character trait, and other narrative component should be justified, explicitly or implicitly, by other elements in the film. The lack of such justification is commonly referred to by Hollywood practitioners as a 'hole'.[5]

It would not be unfair, then, to argue that narratives in Mamet's films contain a number of such 'holes', but one must immediately add the proviso that these holes are not the product of sloppy writing or poor narrative construction. Instead, they are the product of meticulously created stories which, nevertheless, do not always provide spectators with clear answers for all the questions posed, something that is certainly the case in *The Spanish Prisoner*.

With narrative in Mamet's cinema often defying the rules of mainstream classical Hollywood narrative, it comes as no surprise that his use of visual style also tends to differ from the dominant classical one. Again the departures are not sweeping, as the filmmaker generally abides by the rules of classical filmmaking, such as continuity editing and unobtrusive camera movement, which create a transparency of style 'so that the viewer attends to the story being told and not to the manner of its telling'.[6] Yet, on several occasions, Mamet's use of style, especially in terms of frame composition but also in terms of camera movement, editing and sound, ceases to be transparent and evokes instead a strong sense of artificiality.[7]

This artificiality, however, fits well with the themes of deceptive appearances and elusive truths as well as with chains of narrative events that do not necessarily link in a neat and tidy manner. The end result is a particularly unsettling – for American cinema, at least – experience, which has been perhaps best expressed in a review of *The Spanish Prisoner* for the *Sunday Times* by Tom Shone, who wrote that the film 'is ingenious but glassily unengaging, like watching a game of chess at a distance of 100 metres'.[8] This clearly underscores the fact that Mamet's firm association with independent and later with 'indie' cinema has given him a platform from which to develop an approach to filmmaking that stands at odds with the dominant mode of film practice, which for most critics still is the classical Hollywood mode.

This uneasy relationship of Mamet's film with the dominant norms of contemporary American cinema has been highlighted by several reviews of the film, which tend to concentrate on the manner in which spectators are consciously impeded from being drawn into the story and from identifying with the characters because of the filmmaker's stylistic and narrative choices. Here is an indicative sample:

- 'all his films as a director have adopted this look-no-hands style: ingenious, labyrinthine artefacts, pulling back from emotional engagement under cover of accomplished black humour', points out Philip Kemp in his review of *The Spanish Prisoner* for *Sight and Sound*;[9]
- 'there is no emotional satisfaction in the climax or triumph in the victory. For Mamet, it doesn't matter who wins but how the game is played', concludes James Greenberg in his review for *Los Angeles Magazine*;[10]
- '[the] film is smoothest and most convincing but it shares with the writer-director's earlier work a passion for self-consciously creating distance, for holding the audience at arm's length, that remains a rarefied taste', contends Kenneth Turan for the *Los Angeles Post*;[11] and
- '[y]ou are never asked to care about Joe's predicament as the certainties of his universe are systematically eradicated. But then this is a playful exercise in twisting plausibility and expectations until they seize up', writes Ryan Gilbey in the *Independent*, continuing, 'there is a scientific detachment about the way Mamet painstakingly explores every algebraic permutation of a scenario that ping pongs between the Kafkaesque and the Hitchcockian'.[12]

And while all the above reviewers emphasise the issue of the spectator's level of (non-)engagement but remain for the most part positive, other reviewers, like Chris Bolton, consider the film a failure for this particular reason. As he writes in *24 Frames per Second*:

> the ultimate failure of *The Spanish Prisoner* is its inability to ever convince us it's anything but a stylised, overly mannered film. In order to involve the audience in any way, a film must seduce us into believing we're seeing real life, depending on the aims of the director . . . few viewers will be able to relate to any of the stiff, deliberate characters onscreen.[13]

If nothing else, all these reviews highlight the fact that *The Spanish Prisoner* does not invite spectators to respond emotionally to the story in the same ways they would be 'forced' to respond to a classical narrative, to a film where clarity of comprehension is at the very core and all questions are neatly answered, as Thompson argued above. The reviews also imply that Mamet's cinematic choices in terms of narrative construction and visual style create a particular, one could say 'anti-classical', aesthetic, which, not surprisingly, invites different emotional responses from viewers. This aesthetic has been the product of a distinct philosophical view that Mamet developed during his work on American stage and which he transferred in his approach to filmmaking. He labelled this approach 'practical aesthetics'.[14]

Practical Aesthetics

In many respects, Mamet developed his particular approach to filmmaking out of necessity. Coming to cinema from the area of theatre, he was fully aware of his ignorance about the visual aspect of the film, while also firmly subscribing to the view that the audience comes to the cinema to see drama, 'to be piqued, to be misled, to be disappointed at times, so that it can, finally, be fulfilled'.[15] As he stated in an essay entitled 'A First Time Film Director:'

> I'm not going to be John Ford or Akira Kurosawa, but I do know the meaning of each of the sequences, having written them, and if I can reduce the meaning of each of the sequences to a series of shots, each of them clean and uninflected (i.e. not necessitating further narration), then the movie will 'work'; the audience will understand the story through the medium of pictures and the movie will be as good or bad as the story I wrote.[16]

The fundamental principle behind the above approach, which, largely, justifies Mamet's use of style, is to 'keep it simple' so that the audience can concentrate on the story.[17] This 'simplicity' has its foundation in Mamet's interpretation and (sometimes radical) appropriation of ideas and concepts expressed primarily in the works of Aristotle, Constantin Stanislavsky and Sergei Eisenstein. Equally importantly, it is also a product of Mamet's persistent endeavours to stress the significance of the script, be it a play or a screenplay, as the central agent in the process of artistic creation – a view that is understandable given his background as a playwright. This view, however, is also controversial as it goes completely against the dominant mode of film production in American cinema, a mode that historically has treated the screenplay as ephemeral, subject to change according to the whims of stars, producers or test screenings.

Although the work of the figures who have inspired Mamet seem too disparate in terms of subject matter, as well as in terms of the respective fields (philosophy, theatre, film) within which they were expressed, they nevertheless share certain fundamental elements. These can be detected in the definition of dramatic structure that Mamet has adopted, that is, as 'an organic codification of the human mechanism for ordering information. Event, elaboration, denouement; thesis, antithesis synthesis, boy meets girl, boy loses girl, boy gets girl; act one, two, three'.[18] This definition of dramatic structure is remarkable in its effective summary and creative mingling of all three theorists' key positions, as Mamet read them:

- the Aristotelian notion of narrative unity in terms of a character's pursuit of a specific goal through a series of incidents that progresses the story;
- the Eisensteinian notion of montage as the juxtaposition of images that create in the mind of the viewer the progression of the story;[19] and
- the Stanislavsky-inspired practice of treating the character as habitual action; and the definition of habitual action as an attempt to accomplish a goal (which mirrors Aristotle's definition).

As it is evident, all three positions point towards a specific arrangement of narrative information on both the macro-level (Aristotle) and the micro-level (Eisenstein, Stanislavsky). Consequently, they lend themselves to dramatic structure, as Mamet has perceived it, as 'an exercise of a naturally occurring need or disposition to structure the world as thesis/antithesis/synthesis'.[20] It is this disposition, the filmmaker believes, that constitutes (or should constitute) the backbone of every script, good or bad, in theatre or cinema, leaving for the writer therefore just one 'simple' task, namely, to exercise his or her craft in 'stat[ing] the problem'.[21] This necessarily means that the script follows an internal logic, which is (or should be) determined only by the hero's actions as those are stated in the pages of the script, irrespective of whether these actions conform to externally imposed views of what is 'realistic' or not.[22] Consequently, whether something in drama is true in real life or not is irrelevant so long as it is pertinent 'to the hero quest *as it has been stated to us*'.[23] It should come, then, as no surprise that the screenplay is invested with such importance in Mamet's filmmaking practice, especially as he is also the writer of the scripts for all his films.

The emphasis on the hero's actions, as stated in the screenplay, can be clearly detected in Mamet's preoccupation with the scene as the foundation for any creative decision. Unlike many contemporary directors whose use of film style starts from 'arranging' the shot because of the possibilities it offers in terms of the use of *mise en scène*, Mamet firmly believes that the starting point for a film should be the scene, as it is only within the scene that a character's actions can be expressed.[24]

True to the above, Mamet breaks or 'blocks' or divides the script into scenes according to the characters' actions. Each scene is characterised by a clear 'through action' or 'through line' which represents unequivo-cally what the main character does, the specific goal(s) he or she tries to achieve on the way to his or her main objective.[25] The clear demarcation of each scene on those grounds helps the filmmaker leave out all that is unnecessary for the progression of the story material and instead concentrate on how to film (and edit) a scene that portrays a very specific action. Consequently, all stylistic choices (set-designing, costumes, props, make-up, hairstyle, lighting, camerawork) are made on the basis of how they promote the actions that define each scene. Mamet has been adamant about this aspect of his filmmaking practice, which again stems from his work in American theatre. As he stated in one of his essays:

Everything which does not put forward the meaning of the play impedes the meaning of the play. To do too much or too little is to mitigate and weaken the meaning. The acting, the design, the direction should all consist only of that bare minimum necessary to put forward the action.[26]

This terse approach to filmmaking, which is clearly evident in *The Spanish Prisoner*, as my discussion of specific scenes from the film will demonstrate, conveniently also dovetails the filmmaker's work with low budgets in small-scale productions, which were defining characteristics of American 'indie' cinema in the mid-to-late 1990s. Equally importantly, however, Mamet's approach to filmmaking justifies the particular stylistic and narrative choices he makes. As his choices are keyed closely to the main ideas and themes put forward by his screenplays, and as his screenplays deal with such themes as deceptive appearances, elusive truths and the shifting nature of identity, it should come as no surprise that his use of visual style will complement perfectly narrative structures that are shifty, unpredictable and deceitful, while also going against dominant conventions of filmmaking, if the story as he stated it in his screenplay demands it.

One could in fact go as far as to argue that Mamet's filmmaking practice reveals the 'bare essentials' of American cinema, nothing more than a medium that was developed for the purposes of storytelling, before this storytelling assumed externally imposed stylistic and narrative rules and conventions that quickly became amalgamated and institutionalised in what critics have called the classical Hollywood cinema. On the other hand, though, it is exactly his films' (often radical) breaks from Hollywood's classicism and their over-dependence on the script's agency in the creation process that have made his cinema so difficult for film criticism to accept. This becomes particularly obvious in several reviews for *The Spanish Prisoner*. For instance, Gaby Williams for the *Guardian* writes that the film's 'dialogue full of stilted interruptions is intended perhaps to lend an air of eerie unreliability and Pinteresque abstraction. But to me it only feels unfilmic;'[27] and leading American film critic David Denby, in his own review of the film for *New York*, calls for Mamet 'to learn to trust the camera more than he does; he has to stop trying to control everything with language; he has to let loose a little and just give in to the fluency, the ease, the free-flowing pleasure of making a movie'.[28]

Behind these criticisms and words of caution, however, lies a thinly disguised hostility towards films whose visual style bears traces of theatrical techniques, especially ones where the emphasis is often placed on dialogue at the expense of more 'cinematic' stylistic techniques.[29] This hostility has its roots in arguments about cinema's specificity as a visual medium and its (supposed) evolution towards an inherently cinematic language that privileges medium-specific techniques as opposed to dialogue, which was seen as belonging to the world of drama and literature. As David Bordwell pointed out:

Most cinephiles were hostile to even these traces of theatrical technique; Chaplin, for all his genius as a performer, was often considered an 'uncinematic' director. Consequently, historians tended to search for stylistic progress in the 'specifically cinematic' domains of camerawork and editing.[30]

With reference to Mamet, one could then argue that films like *The Spanish Prisoner* tend to be treated by the critical establishment with 'suspicion' (as we saw in Chapter 2); as films that refuse to explore the properties of the medium; as films that rely on an obsolete aesthetic, which in this case is partly redeemed by the undoubted power of Mamet's language. In other words, they are perceived as products of a filmmaker who refuses to become 'cinematic', despite the fact that *The Spanish Prisoner* was his fifth film as a writer-director. And while formal experimentation, extreme stylisation and even overt anti-classicism are celebrated by critics when they take place through the use of medium-specific properties (especially elaborate camerawork), they are treated almost as anathema when any relationship with the stage becomes evident.

Indeed, many reviews revel in the opportunity to highlight Mamet's stage background in order to account for *The Spanish Prisoner*'s 'anti-mainstream' aesthetic: 'It is also a very controlled film and its feeling of constructedness reflects the director's alliance with the stage', writes Ruth Barton;[31] while leading film critic Jonathan Rosenbaum has criticised the filmmaker severely for his use of theatrical conventions in his filmmaking, underscoring the view that 'the conventions of establishing everyday reality in film and on the stage are radically different in terms of time as well as space', and that Mamet's persistent adherence to the latter leave him with no alternative but to depend on dialogue as 'the principal medium of his deceptions'.[32]

No wonder, then, that Mamet had to turn to the independent sector in terms of finding a platform for his distinctive cinematic practice. It's now time to examine the filmmaker's choices in *The Spanish Prisoner* and the anti-classical aesthetic effects these convey.

A Sucker Born Every Minute

Approximately an hour into the film and after forty-three scenes, Joe Ross meets the FBI team who will prep him for his imminent meeting with Jimmy Dell. The latter has been identified by Joe and confirmed by FBI agent Pat McCune as the mastermind behind a confidence game designed to dupe the former into handing him his invaluable 'process', which has the form and shape of a large red notebook with drawings, notes and mathematical equations on its pages and which will help a company control the global market. As the FBI team are putting a wire on Joe to keep him under surveillance during the meeting with Dell, an unnamed male FBI agent who seems to be in charge of the operation explains to him the mechanics of the con trick that has been perpetrated by Dell, a trick that is called 'The Spanish Prisoner' and which of course lends the film its title. As he explains the trick's basic premise there is considerable movement in the gentlemen's toilet where the scene takes place. In their attempt to wire him on, several agents and assistants remove Joe's coat and cardigan, lift his shirt up to place the transmitter and gesticulate to each other while Joe is still listening to the explanation of the trick.

Once the male FBI agent explains it, he asks Joe whether he is ready to go through with the plan to catch Dell. Upon Joe's clear confirmation that he is ready to do it, the same FBI agent starts explaining the procedure. Once again, there is considerable movement on screen (a number of shots of Joe still being prepped and listening to the FBI agent's instructions) and off screen (a number of shots when the camera is on the FBI agent explaining the elaborate procedure with the assistants being heard working off screen). Once Joe is wired, one of the FBI assistants helps him to put his cardigan and coat back on again. It is at this point that Joe passes the copy of his ultra-valuable invention to the FBI agent in charge, as otherwise Joe cannot put his coat on. Prior to this shot he had been holding 'the process' at all times.

What follows is a sequence of fifteen shots where the FBI agent continues with the details of the operation before handing back 'the process' to Joe for his meeting with Dell. It is during these shots that 'the process' is switched over, replaced by an identical, empty red notebook, even though protagonist and spectator will not know this for another two scenes. This sequence of fifteen shots, I would argue, both forms the most significant segment of the film and holds the key to understanding Mamet's approach to filmmaking as summarised at the beginning of this chapter. For, the switch of 'the real process' for the fake red notebook never happens or, to be more precise, could not have happened, given:

- the protagonist's spatial position while listening to and interacting with the male FBI agent in the sequence; and

Table 4.1 The switchover of 'the process'

Shot description	'Process' visible to the protagonist	'Process' visible to the spectator
Six medium shots of the FBI agent holding 'the process', placing it on a window ledge next to him and putting his radio on top of it	Yes	Yes
Five medium shots of Joe listening to the FBI agent's instructions	Yes	No
One high-angle shot of 'the process' itself as the FBI agent browses through it to check if it is 'the real thing'	Yes	Yes
One medium close-up shot of Joe questioning a particular instruction given by the FBI agent	Yes	No
One medium close shot of agent McCune from Joe's point of view. At this point Joe has turned his head to the side opposite to where 'the process' is	No	No
One long shot of the room. The agent picks up 'the process' from the window ledge and hands it in to Joe before the operation starts	Yes	Yes

- the spectator's degree of access to the events of the narrative in the given sequence.

More specifically, Table 4.1 contains the content of these fifteen shots and the protagonist's and spectator's access to the spatial position of 'the process'.

As is evident in the table, during these fifteen shots 'the process' is visible by protagonist and spectator in eight shots, while in the six shots of Joe in which 'the process' is not visible to the spectator, it nevertheless is still visible to the protagonist, as it is within his range of vision as this is established in preceding and succeeding shots in the sequence. That leaves only one shot, the one where he has turned his head towards McCune, who is standing on the opposite side of the room to where 'the process' is, to confirm the nature of her mission in the Caribbean (Figures 1 and 2). This shot of McCune, which is marked as a point-of-view shot from Joe's perspective, is the only one in the sequence where 'the process' is not within the range of the protagonist's vision and not visible by the

Figure 1 Joe has turned his head to the direction opposite to where 'the process' is

spectator either. Plausibly, it is only during that particular shot that the switchover could have taken place, as during all other times 'the process' has been firmly within the protagonist's and/or the spectator's sight.

That critical shot, however, lasts exactly 3.5 seconds, which means that the time when 'the process' was 'out of sight' was also 3.5 seconds. The narrative then demands of spectators that they accept that, in 3.5 seconds and with the protagonist within an arm's length, someone lifted the FBI agent's radio, took 'the process', left an identical notebook in its place, put the radio back on top of it and walked away with the precious invention; or the equally implausible alternative that someone opened the iron window from the outside without making any noise and replaced 'the process' with a fake one while placing the radio back on top of it, again in 3.5 seconds.

It is obvious, then, that the switchover took place not only off screen but also at an impossible narrative space and time, creating thus one of the several 'holes' in the narrative that make the film resist the rules of classicism. This is especially so as there is no scene later in the narrative where it is explained when and how the switchover took place (as is the case in similar American films in order for all the questions to be answered). Cinema spectators, who cannot stop the projection and go back to check the details of the sequence, would have no alternative but to assume that there was a point where the actual switchover occurred, but it was subtle enough for them to have missed it. Home video viewers, however, who have the option of rewinding and freezing the frame, would be surprised to discover that no such point existed in the sequence. And although Mamet's screenplay could easily have made Joe have his attention and viewpoint kept away from 'the process' long enough for a more plausible switchover to take place, the actual narrative consciously chooses to follow its own logic rather than be bound by the clarity of comprehension that stamps classical films.

This sequence turns out to be 'problematic' in terms of style too, something that is immediately emphasised by all this mobility and movement within individual frames. Alongside Joe, the male FBI agent and McCune, there are three more people in the small, enclosed space of the toilets in New York's Central Park where the scene takes place. During the discussion between the FBI agent and Joe, people get in and out of individual

Figure 2 The 'critical shot': 'the process' is outside the range of Joe's vision

frames and, as I mentioned earlier, remove clothing items, nod to each other, look off screen, gesticulate, etc. As a matter of fact the actors' movement is so prominent that the spectator has to try hard to concentrate on the FBI agent's simple explanation of the mechanics of the 'Spanish Prisoner' con trick and on the logistics of the plan to use Joe as bait in order to catch Dell. Following the movement on screen and anticipating action off screen, while also concentrating on the dialogue, stretches the spectator's effort to follow the narrative considerably, especially as the editing also becomes faster (the average shot length of the scene is approximately five seconds, dropping to less than four seconds for the duration of the fifteen key shots). In this respect, even if the narrative had offered a clue as to how the switchover took place, it is very likely that the spectator would have missed it, given the difficulty of the task in hand.

As is evident, these stylistic choices work towards effacing the real nature of events (the FBI team does not prepare Joe for his meeting with Dell; instead they are con artists in disguise stealing 'the process' from, literally, under Joe's nose), and in this respect they complement perfectly the themes of deceptive appearances and elusive truths. The spectator, however, does not always remain a victim of the unpredictable logic of the narrative of *The Spanish Prisoner*. As the sequence of fifteen shots finishes with the male FBI agent handing 'the (fake) process' back to Joe, the narrative decides to offer some clues about the real nature of the unfolding events. Contrary to what most reviews tend to argue, the clues are provided not through dialogue and language but through an instance of 'excessive' visual style, in this case through 'excessive' editing.

While the fifteen-shot sequence finishes with a shot where Joe occupies the left side of the frame and the FBI agent the right (Figure 3), the following shot switches their positions in the frame, thus breaking the 180-degree rule (Figure 4). The shot lasts only for two seconds and it is followed by a shot where their respective position on the frame reverts to the previous arrangement (Figure 5). One of the cornerstones of the classical style in general and of continuity editing in particular, the 180-degree rule ensures that the spectator is always aware of his or her (spatial) relationship to the characters and to the narrative material in general. Traditionally, breaches of this rule, which occur rarely in classical cinema, tend to convey a significant shift in narrative development, often foreshadowing future events – in this case that 'something is not right', or there is no reason why the characters' 'switchover' on the frame takes place – and therefore functioning as clues, at least for the cine-literate spectator.

Figure 3 Joe and the FBI agent after the switchover of 'the process'

After this discussion of the scene, one can appreciate why it holds the key to understanding both the film and Mamet's filmmaking process. In terms of the former, by treating the climax of the con trick as narratively insignificant and therefore purposefully choosing not to show it, after spending forty-four scenes setting it up, the film reveals its true objective: to show that the truth is out of reach and that appearances always have the potential to be deceptive. When protagonist and spectator understand a couple of scenes later that 'the process' has been replaced, they are forced to re-evaluate everything – the protagonist is forced to rethink every single interaction he has had from the trip to the Caribbean onwards; the spectator is forced to re-evaluate the whole narrative to the present moment.

In this respect, it does not matter how exactly 'the process' was switched over under the noses of protagonist and spectator alike. What does matter is that both have been placing their trust far too easily – the protagonist in events and characters he knows nothing about (as it happens, the difference between someone who got off a plane and someone who got out of a boat that came from the direction of a plane is vast); the spectator in a film where, to paraphrase Thompson, 'everything is not necessarily motivated, whether in advance or in retrospect'.

Furthermore, the scene reveals one more fundamental characteristic of the film: the importance of off screen space as the space where the truth is destined to remain hidden; a space that is beyond the reach of the protagonist and, of course, the space from which the con artists derive their powers. By refusing to make this space in any way accessible to a protagonist who is actually present in all eighty-one scenes of the film, and by making such a protagonist the spectator's guide in the narrative world, the film makes this space almost equally inaccessible to the spectator, unless he or she picks up clues like the breach of the 180-degree rule I discussed earlier – clues that are created by the visual style and are not available for the protagonist. With the con artists' plans formulated within that particular space, and with the spectator to a large extent oblivious to this, it should come as no surprise that the culmination of the big trick takes place off screen and implausibly – in the same manner that Joe's

Figure 4 In the following shot Joe and the FBI agent have swapped positions in the frame

Figure 5 The two characters' position in the frame has changed yet again in the following shot, creating a dizzying effect

invention would implausibly help a seemingly small corporate entity control the global market and produce profits so great that they could only be seen off screen.[33]

The film's emphasis on off screen space explains further Mamet's stylistic choices. The frames tend to be composed in such a way as to allow the play between what appears but is deceptive and what exists outside the frames and is true. This also justifies the considerable movement within the frames (as characters enter and exit) in a film not characterised by extensive camera movement. Furthermore, as Joe appears in every scene and in the majority of shots, editing also becomes of primary importance, as the film often alternates shots of Joe with shots of events around him; events that he sometimes perceives, sometimes not, and at other times perceives for something that they are not. As Susan Ricci tells him when he thinks she is calling the police, while in actual fact she is calling off sick to stay at home and help him: 'Well, you're always getting it wrong!' Of course the irony is that Susan is neither calling the police nor calling off sick; instead she is moving to the next action of her part in

the con game, so if Joe trusted her and did think that she was calling off
sick, he would once again 'get it wrong'.

With the 'switchover' scene functioning as a blueprint for an understanding of the film, one could then revisit the narrative of *The Spanish
Prisoner* and reinterpret the considerable number of 'holes' as clues that
would help one question the nature of reality in a much deeper way,
irrespective of the fact that the rules of social and/or cultural verisimilitude come on certain occasions under direct attack. For instance,
at the Caribbean airport just before taking the flight back to New York,
Joe passes through the metal detector while holding in his hands the
wrapped parcel that Dell has previously given him to deliver to his
sister – something that could never take place even in the pre-9/11
times when airport security checks were much more relaxed than in
recent times. Susan, on the other hand, is made to pass her red camera
bag through the X-ray machine, and the scene certainly emphasises this
through the protracted movement on the frame. Does this mean that
the airport security guards staffing the metal detectors and the X-ray
equipment are part of the con, in receipt of a bribe to let Joe pass with
parcel in hands? Or is it a case of incompetence in the workplace and/
or negligence while on duty?

While either is plausible in this case, the answer to these questions
(which the spectator might ask) is treated as yet another narratively
insignificant event sacrificed for the sake of the plot. Although Mamet
could have chosen as part of the narrative to have the parcel pass
through the X-ray machine but make its contents visible only to the
spectator and not to the protagonist, without changing anything else in
the rest of the plot, such a choice would none the less have disturbed the
balance in the distribution of narrative knowledge between protagonist
and spectator that informs the film. For Joe and the spectator tend to
know as much as each other, with the latter offered certain subtle clues
about the possibility of 'foul play', but nothing concrete. Placing the
spectator in the position of superior knowledge to the protagonist, even
momentarily, would result in a very different experience for the spectator, as the pleasures the film's restricted narration offers would cease
to exist (especially as con game films like *The Spanish Prisoner* depend
entirely on the use of restricted narration, as I shall discuss in detail in
the final chapter of this book).

The film contains other such scenes that test the rules of social and/or
cultural verisimilitude, and which none the less continue to explore the

shifting nature of the truth while also playing with the spectator's cognitive skills. For instance, in one scene Joe is asked by McCune to give his date of birth on the phone and he tells her that it is 10 December 1962, while a few scenes later, when he is interrogated by the police, one of the detectives presents him with a bank document with his Swiss account details where his date of birth appears as 7 March 1962.

More testing for the mainstream spectator, however, is the scene where Joe first realises that he is in the process of being conned by Dell. Upon identifying the airport sales assistant and Dell's mistress as the same person, Joe steals FBI agent McCune's business card from Susan's souvenir album and calls her to report Dell. The ensuing conversation is arguably the strongest clue to that point that there is a bigger picture and that it might involve other characters besides Dell, including the FBI agent Joe is talking to on the phone:

[Phone ringing]
Joe: Yes! I, I met you in the islands. . .
McCune: In the islands. . .
Joe: I am calling about the man in the islands, the fellow with the seaplane. . .
McCune: The fellow with the seaplane!
Joe: That's right! Yes! Is he the reason why you were down there?
McCune: The fellow with the seaplane who calls himself Julian Dell . . .
Joe: Yes! That's right!
McCune: Give me your date of birth!
Joe: What?
McCune: You heard me.
Joe: Errm . . . December 10, 1962.
McCune: This fellow Dell, are you with him now?
Joe: No.
McCune: All right, I am going to give you an address. You meet me there. Do you have a pencil?
Joe: Yes.
McCune: Come by yourself. Don't talk to the fellow between now and then. All right.[34]

The conversation strikes one as particularly implausible. At no point does Joe offers his name, while equally the FBI agent does not ask for it. And perhaps even more incredibly, FBI agent McCune volunteers information about her mission in the Caribbean to a complete stranger on the phone. Even if the spectator is pushed to accept that she recognises Joe from his opening lines on the phone, a law agent would never share this type of information with a civilian. For Mamet, however, realism is a discourse that should not seek to 'convince', but instead to 'express',[35] irrespective of the potential danger of destroying familiarity and verisimilitude. As he tellingly put in one of his essays:

In devotion to the Scenic Truth the artist gives him- or herself a choice. In discarding the armor of realism he or she accepts the responsibility of making every choice in light of specific meaning – of making every choice assertive rather than protective. For, in this age, to make a 'realistic' choice, to assert that such and such choice was made because it is, in fact, *as it is in life*, is to say no more than that the choice was made in such a way to avoid any potential criticism.[36]

The Spanish Prisoner, however, assaults the conventions of realism and, more importantly in this case, of classicism from two other perspectives with, arguably, more emphatic results. The first of these perspectives is through scenes, sequences and shots that are 'excessive' in meaning. In these sequences, the filmic narration draws particular attention to a specific element (usually something that assumes the form of a clue for understanding narrative events) for both the protagonist's and the spectator's benefit.[37] However, the attention to this element is so close, protracted and obvious that:

1. the spectator tends to view this with suspicion – a possible red herring designed to throw them yet again off course, prompting critic Amy Taubin to write: 'Mamet's basic strategy is to underline the clues so heavily that you can't help second guessing yourself';[38] and
2. it destroys almost entirely the perceived 'autonomy' of the diegetic world from the mechanics of the narration, as it is clear that narration addresses the protagonist and spectator head on, creating moments of great 'excess' which unsettle the spectator's viewing experience.

Arguably, the most excessive of such scenes occurs towards the end of the film when Joe eventually realises that he still has the original tennis book Dell had given him with the latter's fingerprints on it. He could therefore bring that book to the police and eventually discover Dell's real identity in this manner, rather than through going back to St Estephe in the Caribbean and asking for the hotel security tapes that have captured

Dell while on the island. The scene lasts for a little over two minutes
and starts with a shot of a queue of people in front of a check-in desk at
Boston Airport. Joe and Susan join the queue, with the latter advising
him to look for other evidence besides the security tapes while on the
island, especially things Dell might have touched. Coincidentally, in
front of them there is a woman holding a young boy and pushing a pram
with great difficulty while at the same time asking her son not to leave his
fingerprints on his book.

A couple of shots later the young boy drops his book, with the camera
focusing on the book on the floor. Joe picks it up and passes it to the boy's
mother. Seeing that the book's spine is torn, the woman starts telling off
her son for having damaged his book. At this point, the clues are sufficient and evident enough for the spectator to remember that Joe still has
the original copy of the book he was asked to carry and he had clumsily
torn. But the protagonist has not picked up on this yet. In the next shot
an air stewardess helps the woman with the child to the front of the
queue, while Joe seizes the opportunity to jump ahead of the queue and
volunteers to carry the woman's luggage. As they walk, the woman once
again tells her son off for having torn his book and says she will refuse to
buy him a new one. As the shot changes they are in front of the X-ray
machine, ready to put her hand luggage through. The woman repeats
that the boy has torn his book and that he will not get another one. Then
a number of quick shots take place in which the luggage is going through,
Joe is asked to put his camera through the machine, and the airport security employee tries to calm the restless boy, while ambient airport noise
gives the scene a strange, distant feel. All these shots make Joe's failure
to pick up on the clue even more protracted and prolonged.

These shots are followed by a close-up of the woman with the boy in
her arms saying 'you got your fingerprints all over the book; you've torn it
and you've got your fingerprints all over it'. The dialogue is carried over
in the following shot, where Joe finally pays attention to what the woman
is saying and remembers that he has a book with Dell's fingerprints. He
even repeats the above phrase himself, twice, realising that the solution
to his problem was with him all along. By the end of the scene the word
'book' has been uttered eight times and the words 'torn' and 'fingerprints'
five times each, prompting reviewers to question the scene's 'crude-
ness'. 'The bit about the fingerprints is so deliberate', a critic writes, that
'Mamet should have written the secret in red ink right on the film in case
one or two idiots in the back of the theatre had fallen asleep.'[39]

This excess, moreover, makes spectators not only doubt the nature of the clue (whether it is yet another red herring) but also question the chosen mode of narration for its directness. This is especially so in the light of yet another clear reference to the significance of fingerprints the narration has drawn attention to when, a few scenes earlier, Klein, Joe's boss, pleads with him to return 'the process', while Joe is standing in front of a poster with the word 'fingerprints' in a prominent position.

If scenes like these (with their highly unusual narration) problematise the spectator's relationship to the narrative – a relationship which in mainstream American cinema has traditionally depended on a series of stylistic choices that work towards effacing the presence of narration in order for the spectator to concentrate on the story and not on how the story is told – the actors' mode of performance makes this relationship almost impossible in *The Spanish Prisoner*. More than any other element in Mamet's films, performance, especially the mode of dialogue delivery, comes across as particularly stylised, making spectators, especially ones not familiar with Mamet's work, question anew their experience of his films. One could argue that dialogue delivery in Mamet's film is so markedly different from the average contemporary American film, mainstream or independent, that it is impossible for it to go unnoticed.

At the core of such a performance is the actors' particular manner of uttering the words of the script, which many critics have described as 'emotionless' or 'flat' for want of a better description.[40] Consider for instance Kenneth Turan's description of performance in *The Spanish Prisoner*:

Mamet demands that actors recite words with distancing rhythms and cadences that make the conversations sound as if they took place on [*sic*] an alternative universe that parallels but does not connect to our own. This alienating verbal style puts peculiar emphasis on phrases like 'you're a real gent' and 'I'm loyal and true and I'm not hard to look at' emphasising the artificiality of the situations and making any kind of involvement with the characters hard to imagine.[41]

Whether emotionless, flat or appropriate for an alternative universe, such a mode of delivery seems to allow Mamet's words to maintain their inherent sonic force, as if the importance lies with the words uttered and not with how they are uttered. This distinct mode of dialogue delivery has its roots in Constantine Stanislavsky's 'system' and in the ways in which Mamet interpreted it and attempted to transport it to the medium of cinema. According to Mamet, Stanislavsky's 'system' strove 'to *free* the actor from extraneous considerations and permit him or her to turn his

or her concentration to the objective, which [was] not "this performance" but the *meaning* of the play'.[42] Like the other Stanislavskian concept
of the 'Scenic Truth', which needs to be foregrounded by stylistic choices
that do not necessarily conform to dominant conventions, the 'system'
was seen by Mamet as an approach to acting that starts, again, from the
meaning of the play and not from external notions, such as how the actor
interprets the character, that other Staninslavsky-influenced approaches
such as the 'method' preached.[43]

This approach to performance in the theatre, however, is in direct
contrast to the ways in which Hollywood cinema has traditionally dealt
with questions of performance. As Maltby and Craven argued, acting in
American cinema has traditionally relied on notions of 'sincerity', 'truth'
and 'transparency',[44] and consequently has never had any particular
consideration about central ideas and scenic truths that any screenplay
might suggest.[45] This necessarily means that any attempt to transport
Stanislavsky's system (in the ways Mamet understood it) to the American
cinema would go against a long-standing tradition of acting based on
predominantly realist conventions as these are defined and understood
in different historical periods. This explains why acting in *The Spanish
Prisoner* and in other Mamet films strikes one immediately as artificial,
even though its philosophy and principles are organically linked to the
other elements that constitute Mamet's filmmaking practice.

On the other hand, though, and since the central premise of the story
revolves around a swindle and the artificial world that Joe inhabits,
one could argue that the (seeming) artificiality of acting complements
perfectly the story of the film as well as Mamet's often clichéd and consciously stereotypical language. As a matter of fact, the film is so full of
clichéd proverbs, unfinished sentences and instances of alliteration that
a more 'mainstream' approach to acting might have destroyed its convincing unity of form and content. But since performance in *The Spanish
Prisoner* differs so substantially from performance in mainstream films,
it does draw attention to itself despite its organic unity with the film's
narrative structure and visual style.

Conclusion

As has been evident, *The Spanish Prisoner* differs from the average mainstream film in fundamental ways, while it will not be unfair to suggest
that its stylistic and narrative properties are so distinctive that they

make it stand out in the 'indie' sector too. Working outside the confines of Hollywood allowed Mamet to transport a distinct aesthetic view he developed in theatre to the medium of cinema. The result was a film that, at first sight, looks 'stagy' and contrived and evokes a strong sense of constructedness, both in terms of narrative structure and in terms of visual style and acting. However, as the chapter has argued, this type of film style has been used to support a story that deals essentially with the themes of illusion and artificiality, as it revolves around an elaborate confidence game that a gang of tricksters play with the film's protagonist. In this respect, the film's style clearly emanates from the story itself and therefore becomes an integral aspect of the story's materialisation on the screen. And while for many critics the film 'is far too cerebral to have a heart',[46] for others it stands tall as a real alternative to Hollywood when it comes to commercial cinema, and its filmmaker represents an artist who refuses to succumb to dominant notions of what constitutes good filmmaking:

The reason Mamet pulls this off and turns out a film that is both cinematic and completely oppositional to everything Hollywood stands for at the moment is because of the utter confidence with which he films his script. Never for a moment does the film suggest that there is any better way to tell this story and never for a moment, even at its most ludicrous, does it take itself anything but seriously.[47]

A significant part of its power, though, stems from the rules of the film genre in which *The Spanish Prisoner* belongs, which are examined in the next and final chapter.

5. Playing with Cinema:
The Master of the Con Game Film

A Mamet film requires faith: Things are rarely what they seem. His works are exercises in metamorphosis. Or in illusions. Take your pick.[1]

Introduction

In her book *Weasels and Wisemen: Ethics and Ethnicity in the Work of David Mamet*, Leslie Kane argues that 'game-playing as structure and element of plot is a controlling figure' in both Mamet's films and his stage plays.[2] Following Thomas M. Leitch, who studied the function of game-playing in the films of Alfred Hitchcock, Kane suggests that game-playing in Mamet's films 'evokes complex concordances from which the audience derives pleasure "from having followed the director's lead"'.[3] She continues:

Mamet's films, like Hitchcock's, 'beguile audiences' enticing them to follow the action as 'a move in the game' that surprises or disorients them, 'encourag[ing] them to fall into misidentifications and misinterpretations which have specific moral or thematic force'.[4]

Besides evoking what has once been called 'the master image for genre criticism', an image which in Tom Ryall's words consists of 'a triangle composed of artist/film/audience',[5] the above approach to Mamet's films flirts with genre criticism in, at least, two additional ways. First, it groups a number of films on the basis of a 'controlling' common characteristic (in this case game-playing). Second, it raises the question of the spectators' systems of expectations in the viewing process and the way in which those systems are affected by the controlling characteristic of this group of films (spectators are encouraged to misidentify and misinterpret). If this is true for all Mamet films, it is never more so than for *The Spanish Prisoner*, a film that, according to critics, 'twists and turns more than the *Tour de France*' and proves to be a 'bewildering experience'.[6]

In the light of such strong claims about the existence of a generic framework within which *The Spanish Prisoner* can be located, the final chapter of this book sets out to examine the framework in question, to map out its main features and, generally, to address questions of genre in an 'indie' film like this one. More specifically, this chapter concerns itself with introducing and defining a film genre hitherto unrecognised by film criticism. This genre, which I would like to call the 'con artist film', and its important subcategory, the 'con game film', have had a long-standing institutional history within American cinema – with the lion's share of such films located in the post-1970 Hollywood cinema. However, its critical recognition and appreciation have remained remarkably elusive.

Instead, the apparatus of film criticism (popular and scholarly) has resorted consistently to more established genre labels, categories and other appellations which, more often than not, were clearly overstretched in their attempt to 'include' films that, as I will argue, belong primarily to a different generic group, the con artist and the con game film. These labels have included the 'crime film' and one of its subcategories, the 'suspense thriller',[7] to classify films such as *Confidence* and *The Spanish Prisoner*, respectively; the 'neo-noir film' to describe *House of Games*, *The Grifters*, and *The Spanish Prisoner* and *Confidence* again; and the 'caper film' to characterise *Matchstick Men*; while a film like *Traveller* has been discussed as a 'comedy-adventure' and a 'comedy-drama'.[8]

This chapter, then, attempts to put the record straight by introducing and defining the con artist and the con game film before identifying *The Spanish Prisoner* as arguably the quintessential example of the latter. Specifically, the chapter will chart a brief institutional history of a representative corpus of films by looking at the discourses that have surrounded their advertising and marketing, which, according to Lukow and Ricci, are collectively called the films' 'inter-textual relay'.[9] The chapter will then move to examine briefly the films' style, internal structure, motifs, narrative trajectories and the horizon of expectations they invite spectators to form, before examining in detail the subcategory of the con game film, laying the ground for a constructive discussion of the generic properties of *The Spanish Prisoner*.

Genre Recognition (1): The Industrial/Institutional Context

Defining the con

CON: Abbrev. of CONFIDENCE. Used *attrib.* in *con game, man, talk*, etc. (Also *ellipt.*) orig. *U.S.* (*Oxford English Dictionary Online*)

In order to introduce the con artist film as genre, one needs to start from the word 'con' and its semantic qualities. Although the word 'con' as an abbreviation of 'confidence' and a prefix to the word 'man' ('con man') became popular in the late nineteenth century, it has nevertheless had a much longer presence in its full, unabbreviated format. What comes immediately to mind is Herman Melville's *The Confidence Man: His Masquerade* (originally published in 1857), a novel that deals with a trickster who exposes the greed and shallowness of the (then) contemporary American society. In the introduction to the Penguin edition of the novel (1990), Stephen Patterson writes that the phrase 'confidence man' was coined in 1849 by the *New York Herald* to report the activities of one 'William Thompson', 'a man with a variety of aliases'.[10] Although the figure of the confidence man had already been present in European life and was introduced in literature before 1849, Patterson suggests that 'it was the Americans who gave him "a local habitation and a name"'. This was mainly because American people have always had a fascination with confidence artists, a fascination that stemmed from their 'emphasis on and admiration for individual enterprise and ingenuity, which [were] considered notably "Yankee" qualities'.[11]

According to the *Oxford English Dictionary*, one of the first uses of the word as an abbreviation of 'confidence' and as a prefix to the word 'man' was noted in *Mercury*, a Portland newspaper, in 1889. The sentence, which is cited in the dictionary, reads: 'It does not take an unsophisticated countryman to get swindled by the "con man."'[12] This clearly sets the foundations for the subsequent use of the word 'con' as a synonym for 'cheating' and 'deceit', words which, in actual fact, stand as antonyms for the original word 'confidence'. This paradox is further reinforced when the word 'con' is used on its own, as in an article in *The Listener* (21 December 1967), which featured the sentence 'The intellectual theoreticians of visual pop culture have succeeded . . . in pulling a con.'[13] In this context 'con' becomes a synonym for 'trick' and/or 'illusion', and once again dispenses with the original meaning of the word it stems from.

What becomes evident from the above two literary examples is the negative connotations of the word. In both cases, the perpetrators of the 'con' are presented as individuals or groups of people who are capable of fooling other people (as in the first example) or of putting across a view that does not hold true but which none the less becomes accepted as true (as in the second example). In other words, both subjects achieve a goal by indirect means and at the expense of an object (in the syntactical sense) who assumes the position of the victim.

Finally, the *Oxford English Dictionary* features a further example of the use of the word 'con', this time from J. B. Priestley's *Festival at Farbridge*. The novel in question features a line of dialogue which can be easily used as a definition for the term 'con artist' for the purposes of this chapter: 'You're a little gang of crooks, con types living on your wits.'[14] Here the phrase 'con types' suggests a particular type of criminal (or criminals) who earn(s) a living by applying certain skills based on their wits. The use of wit as the weapon of choice for these criminals differentiates them from other 'common' crooks who use guns, physical violence or any other type of force to extract money or valuable goods from their victims. It is this eschewing of violence that will prove critical in establishing a distinct identity for the genre of the con artist film.

With this definition in mind, I am now turning my attention to the place of the con in American cinema, paying particular attention to a number of films that feature con artists as protagonists and con games as an integral part of their narrative structure and the way these have been promoted and advertised. As this is potentially a mammoth task (because it involves an examination of all the literature that accompanies the release of a film not only in the United States but, significantly, in the other countries where a film is exhibited), I will mainly concentrate on only two of the marketing strategies that all distributors use in the advertising of their films: the film title and the tagline. I will also consider how *Variety*, the main trade publication for American cinema, has reviewed those films – what generic frameworks have been assigned to these film. What I shall demonstrate is that despite the reluctance of *Variety* reviewers to identify such films as primarily con artist films, the term 'con' and the other words belonging to the same semantic field ('swindle', 'scam' and 'scheme', in particular) have had an established and, in recent years, prominent history in the discourses of marketing and advertising that surrounded those films. This clearly supports an argument for the existence of the generic categories of the con artist and con game films. Once this history is charted, I shall approach the genre from a critical perspective.

The Con in American Cinema

Films that feature con artists as protagonists and narratives revolving or structured around the perpetration of scams and confidence games have existed from the earliest days of American cinema. As far back as 1905, *Green Goods Man; or Josiah and Samanthy's Experience with the Original 'American Confidence Game'* (Vitagraph) dealt with a couple's experience with a con man when they leave their home in the village and come to the city; and in 1911, *Get Rich Quick* (Thanhouser) dealt with the effects of a scam performed by the 'Utopia Investment Corporation' on its victims. Since then the character of the con artist has featured regularly in American films, with key examples including *The Small Town Guy* (Windom, 1917, George Kleine System, US); *The Last of Mrs Cheney* (Franklin, 1929, MGM); *Beg Borrow or Steal* (Thiele, 1937, MGM); and, perhaps the best known of all, *The Lady Eve* (P. Sturges, 1941, Paramount). These films, however, were not advertised as con artist films, as neither their title nor the publicity surrounding them drew explicit attention to that particular element of them.

In 1951, however, there was one of the earliest uses of the word 'con' in this context, in the publicity material accompanying the release of *Merry Mavericks*, a film starring the Three Stooges. The film's tagline, which reads 'Meet The Three Stooges as up-and-coming . . . always leave-'em-laughing con-men in the wild and woolly west!', makes concrete references to two established generic categories: comedy ('leave-'em-laughing') and the western ('wild and woolly west'), alongside the non-established con artist one.[15] However, it is the brand name 'The Three Stooges' that is the actual focal point of the tagline, thanks to its place in the sentence at the very beginning and, more importantly, to the specific connotations of comedy it implies. With the title of the film also clearly suggesting a comedy, it is not surprising that the phrase 'con-men' becomes squeezed in the tagline, sandwiched between the other two more dominant generic contexts.

This early example of the way distributors have dealt with a film that features con men is indicative of the problems associated with the institutional recognition of the con artist and the con game film, if not as a genre, at least as a type of film with a distinct identity. The majority of films featuring plots about cons, scams and swindles have been consistently marketed as films that, primarily, belong to a different, more established, film genre

Table 5.1 American film taglines containing the word 'con'

Title	Year	Tagline
Shooting Fish	1997	As con artists they were hard to beat. But they were easy targets for LOVE
The Distinguished Gentleman	1992	From con man to congressman
Diggstown	1992	Where the pros meet the cons
Bullseye!	1990	They were the world's greatest conmen . . . Almost.
Doc Hooker's Bunch	1976	His gang of female flim-flammers con their way across the old West!
The Barefoot Mailman	1951	Meet Sylvanus! Con man . . . Gun man . . . Ladies' man

Source: www.imdb.com

or genres and then as films that feature specific types of characters or plots that the terms 'con artist film' and 'con game film' might suggest. Table 5.1 offers some examples of films whose tagline contains the word 'con' but which were mainly advertised as films belonging to different genres.

As it is evident from the taglines in Table 5.1, *The Distinguished Gentleman, Diggstown* and *Bullseye!* have been marketed primarily as comedies, *Shooting Fish* as romance and *Doc Hooker's Bunch* as a comedy-western, while *The Barefoot Mailman* seems to be advertised as a mix of genres including gangster/adventure, romance and, of course, con artist film. This pattern would suggest that the con artist and con game film do not exist as distinct industrial categories in the distribution process of American films. Yet the category is never completely marginalised in the advertising of films (in this case film title and tagline) that feature such characters or narrative situations.

In recent years, however, there have been a number of American films where the dominant or only generic framework seems to involve primarily conning, deceiving, cheating and (non-)trusting, and which therefore have a potential interest for the con artist film category. Table 5.2 lists such films. Although it does not claim to be exhaustive, the list nevertheless contains a good sample of titles. The titles in bold are further discussed later as characteristic examples of con artist and con game films, and words in the films' taglines that draw attention to questions of conning have also been highlighted in bold.

Even though some of these films employ the character of the con artist in different ways and their narratives might be structured around

Table 5.2 American films of potential interest for the con artist film genre

Title	Year	Tagline
The Artists	2006	Out of Hollywood, Out of Work, and Out To Pull The Perfect **Scam**
The Honeymooners	2005	Dream Big. **Scheme** Bigger
The Big Bounce	2004	It's all in who you **trust**
Criminal	2004	Ever get the feeling of being **played**?
Matchstick Men	2003	Lie **cheat** steal rinse repeat
Confidence	2003	Four bit time **swindlers** . . . who will outsmart whom?
Behind the Nine	2003	**Trust** . . . is overrated
Tough Luck	2003	There's a **sucker** born every minute.
Under the Influence	2002	Murder, **deceit**, fraud . . . another perfect day in Los Angeles.
Catch Me If You Can	2002	The true story of a real **fake**.
Where the Money Is	2000	Another **con**. Another sting. Another day.
Bowfinger	1999	The **con** is on.
The Talented Mr Ripley	1999	It's better to be a **fake** somebody than a real nobody
The Last Call	1998	Ultimately, the **con game** will make you very rich or very dead . . . probably both.
The Spanish Prisoner	1997	It's the oldest **con** in the book.
Traveller	1997	Swindlers. **Scam**mers. Con-men. As American as apple-pie.
Bound	1996	A **trust** so deep it cuts both ways.
Deadfall	1993	You won't know who to **trust**. What to believe. Or where to turn.
Glengarry Glen Ross	1992	Lie. **Cheat**. Steal. All In A Day's Work.
The Grifters	1990	Seduction. Betrayal. Murder. Who's **Conning** Who?
House of Games	1987	Human Nature Is A **Sucker** Bet
The Sting II	1983	The **con** is on . . . place your bets!
Charleston	1977	Charleston is my name. **Con trick**s are my game!
The Day the Lord Got Busted	1976	The Greatest **CON MAN** of them all!
Paper Moon	1973	As P.T. Barnum put it, 'There's a **sucker** born every minute.'
The Sting	1973	. . . all it takes is a little **Confidence**.
The Great Impostor	1961	Will the Real Fred Demara Please Stand Up??

confidence tricks to various degrees, one can, none the less, clearly detect a pattern in the films' advertising. This pattern certainly suggests the possibility of a trend within recent (especially post-1990) American film production and, of course, the existence of a specific generic framework. In particular, the taglines of the films in Table 5.2 invite spectators to form specific expectations, the most important of which seem to be the following:

1. to be aware of the many directions that narrative trajectories might take (e.g. *The Grifters, Deadfall, Confidence* and *Under the Influence*);
2. to expect byzantine and labyrinthine plots which are structured around characters who cheat, lie and betray and around the consequences of such actions; and, less prominently,
3. to perceive those films as a 'slice of Americana', a typical day in American life (e.g. *Traveller, Matchstick Men, Glengarry Glen Ross, Under the Influence*).

This system of expectations, however, does not necessarily differentiate potential con artist and con game films from other categories of film or genres, especially the suspense thriller and the crime film (genres that habitually depend on the spectator's expectations of many of the above elements) and does not therefore automatically signal a distinct film genre within American cinema. In fact, most of the films in the list can potentially be seen as belonging to the thriller or crime film genres (and for the vast majority of critics they do), both established genres with a much longer and prominent institutional history. In order to establish a distinct identity for at least some of the films in Table 5.2, I will proceed to examine a further advertising strategy that distributors routinely use in film marketing. This is, admittedly, one that has rarely been examined as such, namely the choices distributors make when they translate the title of a film for non-English-speaking audiences. What will become evident is that the titles of a significant number of films from Table 5.2 have actually been translated (into French, Italian, German, Spanish and Greek) in a manner that is much more clearly suggestive of their content as films about con artists/con games. Table 5.3 offers seven such examples.

What is instantly apparent is the emphasis international distributors place on the central characters of the films as con artists and swindlers (*Matchstick Men* in Spanish and Greek; *Traveller* in French; *The Grifters* in French, Spanish and Greek). Furthermore, there is an equally prominent tendency to highlight the con or swindle itself (*Matchstick Men* in Italian and German; *The Spanish Prisoner* in Italian, German, Spanish and Greek; *House of Games* in Greek; and *The Sting* in French, German and Spanish),

Table 5.3 Translations of con artist films in different languages

English	French	Italian	German	Spanish	Greek
Confidence 2003	*Confidence* (original)	*Confidence* (original)	*Confidence* (original)	*Confidence* (original)	*Akros embisteftiko* [Highly Confidential]
Matchstick Men 2003	*Les Associes* [The Associates]	*Il Genio della Truffa* [The Genius of the Swindle]	*Tricks* [Tricks]	*Los impostores* [The Impostors]	*Epagelmaties apateones* [Professional Swindlers]
The Spanish Prisoner 1997	*La Prisonnière Espagnole* (literal)	*La Formula* [The Formula]	*Die Unsichtbare Falle* [The Invisible Trap]	*La trama* [The Plot]	*Stimeno Paihnidi* [Set Up Game]
Traveller 1997	*Les Truands* [The Crooks]	*Traveller* (original)	*Traveller* (original)	*Traveller* (original)	not available
The Grifters 1990	*Les Arnaqueurs* [The Swindlers]	*Rischiose Abitudini* [Risky Habits]	*Grifters* (original)	*Los timadores* [The Con Men]	*Kleftes* [The Thieves]
House of Games 1987	*Engrenages* [The Chain of Events]	*La Casa dei Giochi* (literal)	*Haus der Spiele* (literal)	*La casa de los juegos* (literal)	*I leshi tis apatis* [The Club of Deceit]
The Sting 1973	*L'Arnaque* [The Swindle]	*La stangata* (literal)	*Der Clou* [The Hit]	*El golpe* [The Hit]	*To kentri* (literal)

giving away the subject of the films. The titles' emphasis on the central character type in the above films is not coincidental. All seven titles in the table feature central characters who are con artists by profession. These characters occupy the position of the protagonist in four films (*Confidence*, *Traveller*, *The Grifters* and *The Sting*), that of the antagonist in two films (*House of Games* and *The Spanish Prisoner*) and both positions in one film (*Matchstick Men*).

If the profession of the central characters in these films is not a sufficiently strong factor (compared for instance to the profession of the central protagonists in gangster films) to label the above films as con artist films, the international distributors' tendency to highlight the con in the translation of the titles seems to be a stronger factor. For each film from Table 5.3 is indeed structured around a number of con games either as standalone scams (*The Grifters, Traveller*) or as part of one long, elaborate, master con game (*Confidence, Matchstick Men, The Spanish Prisoner, House of Games, The Sting*). Consequently, the distributors' marketing strategy of highlighting this element suggests a distinct identity – at least in terms of content – for the above group of films and, potentially, the existence of a master generic framework within which these films can be primarily located.

Despite the above evidence, however, the intertextual relay of these films consists also of conflicting discourses that effectively question the existence of such a master generic framework. Instead, they highlight an alternative generic context or even a mix of contexts which are not always convincing (and occasionally completely contradictory). The discourses created by trade and press reviews, in particular, seem to be firmly opposed to the idea of the con artist and con game film as adequate descriptive labels, despite frequent references to cons, scams, swindles, schemes and con men within the written text, as the following extracts from reviews that appeared in *Variety* clearly indicate. The reviews' references to genre have been highlighted in bold while the references to cons, swindles, scams, etc. as well as to elements in the review that support the existence of con artist/con game genre have been italicised:

[*Confidence*] is a stylish compelling **crime caper** full of smoothly navigated plot twists . . . Foley's polished direction and Jung's clever script expertly stack enough *multiple deceptions and surprise turnabouts* to keep the action ticking. The increasingly *complex mechanics of the scheme* are elaborated with clarity and dexterity and the audience is kept guessing about the trustworthiness and loyalties of the shifty characters.

Matchstick Men is a **coldly crafty character piece** about some seriously quirky LA *scam artists* . . . [The] script feels like a companion piece to the sorts of *Catch Me If You Can*. . . When the *scam unravels at the last minute* . . . revelations as to who's really been *conning* whom all along . . . [The film] never really casts off its cloak of *artificiality* and calculation.

David Mamet has a penchant for **sleight of hand thrillers**, and *The Spanish Prisoner* is his craftiest to date. Centered on *a relentless cat's cradle of a business scam*, the picture is a devilishly clever series of *reversals* that keeps you guessing to the very end . . . [*The Spanish Prisoner*] is the sort of daunting, satisfying **thriller**, one would like to see several times just to be sure one hasn't missed any clues or *reverses*. A beautifully crafted **noir**, it's an airtight entertainment sure to sate any audience that wants to be engaged, *challenged and surprised*.

Traveller concerns a tight knit clan of con men with a strict subculture and truly bizarre mores . . . [One of its sections] pretty much follows a **Hollywood buddy movie** format . . . In the manner of *familiar Hollywood yarns about con artists*, the film humanizes its protagonists . . . Well executed climax involves a *scheme* in which . . . trying to *outsmart* a wealthy mobster and his dangerously vicious men . . . *Predictably, the scam goes awry.*

Producer Martin Scorsese and director Stephen Frears may have had the ideal sensibility for this [*The Grifters*] **quirky tale of deception and erotic gamesmanship** . . . Donald Westlake's script sticks to the form and spirit of Thompson's **underworld** narrative.

Writer David Mamet's first trip behind the camera as a director is entertaining good fun, an **American film noir** with **Hitchcockian touches** and a few dead bodies along the way. His *big con involves an elaborate set up* to convince a conventioneer, picked up by partner Mike Nussbaum, to offer 'security' for a suitcase full of money found on the street. *House of Games* cleverly selects its *cons*, explain their workings, then *twists them around again*, all without boring or losing the viewer.

The Sting: Outstanding **con game film**. Paul Newman and Robert Redford are superbly re-teamed, this time as *a pair of con artists* in Chicago of the 30s . . . George Roy Hill's outstanding direction of David S. Ward's *finely-crafted story of multiple deceptions and surprise ending* will delight both mass and class audiences . . . The 127 minute film comes to *a series of startling climaxes, piled atop one another with zest*. In the final seconds the *audience realises it has been had*, but when one enjoys the ride, it's a pleasure.[16]

With the exception of the review for *The Sting*, the rest of the *Variety* reviews clearly highlight the problems involved when it comes to attaching genre labels to films featuring con artists and con games. In particular, films such as *The Grifters, Traveller* and *Matchstick Men* seem to resist firmly traditional generic classification, so much so that the reviewer has to resort to vague and rather meaningless phrases such as 'character piece' (*Matchstick Men*) and 'quirky tale of deception and erotic gamesmanship' (*The Grifters*). Reviewers also tend to focus on only one section of a film which seems to fit within an established genre such as 'the buddy movie' (*Traveller*). Furthermore, Mamet's films are characterised by the trade journal as thrillers with noir tones (*The Spanish Prisoner*) or, conversely, as film noir with Hitchcockian thriller tones (*House of Games*).

These labels seem too broad and general to classify the two films meaningfully, given that both labels attached are composites of the same two genres, one of which (the thriller) can be further subdivided into a number of smaller, more meaningful categories such as 'the thriller of murderous passions, the political thriller, the thriller of acquired identity, the psychotraumatic thriller, the thriller of moral confrontation and the innocent-on-the-run-thriller' – none of which could be satisfactorily applied to *The Spanish Prisoner*, as I will discuss later.[17] This leaves *Confidence* as the only example of a film where a specific but questionable generic label ('crime caper') is attached.

On the other hand, these *Variety* reviews consistently refer to the use of specific plot conventions, narrative situations, set pieces and trajectories (see italicised words and phrases in the above reviews). This is the case to such an extent that a *Variety* reader who has not seen the above films would be forgiven for thinking that they belong to a certain group of films with several common elements, had the reviews not featured the problematic genre labels mentioned above. The reviews, furthermore, frequently raise the question of the spectator's systems of expectations regarding the above films. These systems seem to be structured predominantly around the elements of mystery and surprise as the spectator is invited to guess the narrative trajectory in a group of films where multiple narrative twists and reversals are among the dominant structural components.

More importantly for the purposes of this chapter, however, two particular reviews (*The Sting* and *Traveller*) make explicit references to 'con game film' and 'familiar Hollywood yarns about con artists' respectively (even though the review for *Traveller* refuses to label the film in question as such). These phrases acknowledge the presence of a specific generic framework that is waiting to be defined and extrapolated. In support of this statement one could also add a number of extra-textual connections between the above films, connections that can be noted in other promotional material and further encourage their grouping under the umbrella terms 'con artist film' and 'con game film'.

For instance, in 'Anatomy of a Scene' (a special feature produced by the Sundance Channel and accompanying the release of *Confidence* on DVD in the US), Doug Jung, screenwriter of the film, admits that he was influenced by *House of Games* and *The Sting*.[18] In the Production Notes for *Traveller* (one of the special features included in the film's release on DVD in the US), Bill Paxton, producer and star of the film, likens his part to Joe Mantegna's Mike in *House of Games* and John Cusack's Roy in *The Grifters*.[19] The *Variety* review for *Matchstick Men* compares the film to *Catch Me If you Can* and *Paper Moon*, two other films that feature con artists as protagonists. Finally, a *Screen International* feature on James Foley, director of *Confidence*, actually puts on paper the words that none of the above reviewers – with the exception of the *The Sting* – wants to utter when it opens with the phrase: 'When it came to attaching a director for *ensemble con man drama Confidence*, James Foley almost picked himself.'[20]

All the above evidence points towards the existence of a group of films which also seem to be conscious of the existence of their predecessors on a textual level (for instance, the protagonist of *Matchstick Men* and *The Grifters* has the same name, Roy; the main female character's name in *Confidence* and *The Grifters* is Lily; *The Spanish Prisoner* pays homage to *The Sting* by featuring a scene with a merry-go-round; and so on). In the light of this, the chapter moves on to establish this group of films as a distinct genre and discuss *The Spanish Prisoner* as a representative film.

Genre Recognition (II): The Critical Context

Perhaps the biggest problem in critically establishing a distinctive categorical identity for the con artist film lies in its ties with other genres, such as the crime film and the (suspense) thriller – particularly with the former. This problem (which also exists on an institutional level, as the *Variety* reviews demonstrated) expresses itself here mainly in the common-sense view that con artists are criminals and that con tricks constitute a form of crime, irrespective of the facts that the perpetrators of the con do not resort to violence or any other form of physical force to achieve their objective, and that the victims willingly hand their own fortune, property or goods to the con artist. Using false pretences to extract material wealth from unsuspecting people as a profession is illegal and therefore a crime, despite the fact that exactly the same premise is perfectly acceptable (and does not qualify for legal punishment) when it takes place in a non-professional context, as part of everyday life.[21] As films which portray a (particular type of) criminal who performs (particular types of) crime, con artist films are difficult to distinguish from other crime films.

As Steve Neale argued, however, generic specificity:

is not a question of particular and exclusive elements, however defined, but of exclusive and particular combinations and articulations of elements, of the exclusive and particular weight given in any one genre to elements which in fact it shares with other genres.[22]

The questions to ask here, then, are which exclusive and particular combinations of elements are characteristic of the con artist film and how these are articulated. One way of addressing this question is to return to the study that raised it, Steve Neale's seminal *Genre*, and follow one of the central arguments of this book, namely that 'genres are modes of [Hollywood's] narrative system' and that their specificity can be determined by the ways in which they regulate the system's potentiality.[23] According to Neale, different genres articulate, specify and represent equilibrium and disruption (of the equilibrium) in different and differential ways, bringing into play 'a particular combination of particular types or categories of discourse'.[24] By looking, then, at how the equilibrium of a particular narrative order is disrupted, the critic is in a position to start determining the marks of generic specificity as those are articulated 'in terms of conjunctions and disjunctions between a set of discursive categories and operations'.[25] Neale performs this task top-down by assuming that the genre categories he examines (western, gangster, detective, horror, musical, melodrama and comedy films) already exist as genres with distinct identity. I shall be performing the same task here bottom-up, to differentiate a non-established genre category, the con artist film, from an established one, the crime film.

In Neale's view, the western, gangster and detective film are examples of genres where the disruption of equilibrium is 'always figured literally – as physical violence', which also becomes the 'means' by which the disequilibrium will give way to a restored equilibrium, when (social) order is re-established. For this reason, Neale continues, both equilibrium and disequilibrium 'are signified specifically in terms of Law, in terms of the absence/presence, effectiveness/ineffectiveness of legal institutions and their agents'. Consequently, the discourses brought into play by the above genres are discourses about 'crime, legality, justice, social order, civilisation, private property, civic responsibility and so on'. The difference between the above genres exists 'in the precise weight given to the discourses they share in common, in the inscription of these discourses across more specific generic elements and in their imbrication across the codes specific to cinema'.[26]

Neale's approach provides a concrete entry for a discussion of questions pertaining to genre specificity, since it allows critics to start from the genre film itself and work their way to the social aspects of the genre. Furthermore, if one sees the gangster and detective film as subcategories of a broader, more encompassing genre, the crime film (which in Neale's later study *Genre and Hollywood* appears to contain the detective, gangster and suspense thriller film [2000, pp. 71–85]), one can indeed establish the contours specific to the con artist film as both similar to and different from the crime film and its subcategory, the suspense thriller.

Taking the disruption of equilibrium as a starting point in a critical approach to the con artist film, it is easy to detect one fundamental difference from its 'related' genres. Rather than the disruption being marked as physical violence, it is actually marked as a failure in a particular character's cognitive abilities to recognise the truth behind appearances, to distinguish between substance and effect. For this reason, although violence does indeed lurk underneath the shadowy transactions of the con artists with their potential victims, it more often than not expresses itself occasionally and does not necessarily impinge on the trajectory of the narrative. Conversely, the character's attempt to find the truth amidst a web of lies and deceit – in other words to re-establish the proper function of his or her cognitive skills – seems to be a lot more important than recovering his or her money or goods or punishing the perpetrators of the con. A brief survey of how the disruption of the equilibrium is articulated in the films in Table 5.3 will prove the point.

In *Matchstick Men*, Roy (Nicolas Cage) fails to see that the long-lost daughter who suddenly disrupts his life is in fact a con woman who, along with Roy's crime partner and his doctor, have teamed up to con him out of his savings. In *The Spanish Prisoner*, as I shall discuss in detail later, Joe fails to understand that his boss's reluctance to reward him immediately for the invention of 'the process', an act that triggers all the other actions in the narrative, is the first step in an elaborate plan to steal 'the process' from him. In *Traveller*, a film in which the protagonist's (lack of) vision is constantly invoked, Bokky (Bill Paxton) fails to realise that he does not belong to the community of swindlers in which he has spent all his life. In *The Grifters*, Roy (John Cusack) fails to grasp that his mother's efforts towards reconciliation with him are not as deep as he imagines. In *House of Games*, Margaret (Lindsey Crouse) fails to see that Billy, her gambling-addicted client, is in fact working for a gang of con artists and her decision to help him is another first step in an elaborate plan, in this case to con her out of $80,000.

Interestingly, *Confidence* and *The Sting* are the only films in the group where the disruption of equilibrium is actually marked by an act of physical violence (the killing of Big Al in *Confidence*, the killing of Luther in *The Sting*). However, I would like to argue that in both films violence is, in fact, incidental and follows a structurally more important element: the central characters' failure to see that their 'mark' is 'connected' to a crime boss (the King in *Confidence* and Lonnegan in *The Sting*), which of course motivates their violent retaliation. Thus, even though the events following the disruption of the equilibrium in *Confidence* and *The Sting* are to a certain extent driven by Jake's (Ed Burns) and Hooker's (Robert Redford) desire to avenge the death of their partners, this motivation fades away (especially in *Confidence* and to some extent in *The Sting*) as the con game is being set up. Both Henry Gondorf (Paul Newman) and Hooker, and Jake, are immersed in the elaborate trick they are preparing, so much so that in both films the dead member of each gang is mentioned only once more after the opening sequences. Furthermore, neither film ends in the spirit of 'justice is done' which would support the vengeance motive. For all those reasons, it is more useful to perceive the disruption of equilibrium as marked by one or more characters' failure to see reality, with the rest of the narrative exploring the consequences of this failure until order is restored, and not as physical violence which motivates vengeance, as Alan Nadel has argued in his discussion of *The Sting*.[27]

If the disruption of equilibrium in con artist films is marked by the failure of a character's cognitive abilities to perceive the truth behind appearances, then what are the discourses mobilised for the restoration of order and in what specific ways is order restored? Not surprisingly, what becomes immediately apparent (and automatically differentiates the con artist film from other crime films) is that legal institutions and their agents are rarely present. Furthermore, in the few cases where they do appear (FBI agents in *The Sting*, US Customs officers and LAPD detectives in *Confidence*, a police officer in *House of Games*, a US marshal and a police detective in *The Spanish Prisoner*, two patrolmen in *The Grifters*), they are either con artists disguised as agents of the law (*The Sting*, *House of Games*), corrupted officials who demand a cut of the loot and therefore are con artists by proxy (*Confidence*), or narratively insignificant characters (*The Grifters*) who contribute nothing to the restoration of order. This leaves only one film (*The Spanish Prisoner*) where a law agent turns out to be instrumental in the establishment of a new equilibrium, but nevertheless he is perceived as another con man until the final scene of the film, which I shall discuss later.

The overwhelming absence of the legal institutions and their agents clearly suggests that the mobilised discourses have little to do with the discursive categories Neale identified in the crime film, and that consequently one needs to look for them elsewhere. One could argue, therefore, that equilibrium and disequilibrium in con artist films are signified specifically in terms of the healthy function or not of one or more characters' cognitive skills (perception, cognition, comprehension, realisation and recognition). In this respect, the main discourse mobilised in con artist films is that of human nature, which stretches to include psychological, sociological, theological, political, cultural and other perspectives, with particular emphasis on the psychology of the human mind. For instance, in *The Spanish Prisoner* one can discern discursive categories such as the position of 'man' in society (sociological perspective), evident in Joe's effort to secure what he believes is owed to him. One can also detect the discourse of the psychology of the human mind (psychological perspective), which is particularly evident in the sequences when Jimmy Dell tries to teach Joe how people think. Furthermore, there is also the discourse of the culture of greed (cultural perspective), which, of course, permeates the whole film and many others.

On the other hand, while the discursive categories of crime, legality and justice are also mobilised they nevertheless assume a considerably less important role. This is mainly due to the narrative absence or ineffectiveness of the legal institutions and their agents. As a result, these discursive categories are articulated in individual rather than social (legal) terms. Additionally, it is one particular cognitive skill, recognition, that takes on the responsibility of reinstating the new equilibrium, as the narrative trajectories of con artist films tend to culminate in the recognition of (an often important) truth. Again a brief review of the reinstatement of the equilibrium in the above films will prove helpful.

In *Matchstick Men*, Roy recognises that he longs to have the family he had previously not desired only after a con woman disguised as his daughter has awakened his paternal instincts (and in the process conned him out of his money). In *The Spanish Prisoner*, Joe desperately tries to understand why people would want to cheat, steal and lie rather than work for a living, and is left completely alone when it turns out that every person he trusted had participated in a con to steal 'the process' from him. In *Traveller*, Bokky recognises that life outside the clan of 'travellers' is, indeed, possible, while Pat (Mark Wahlberg) takes his position in the clan. In *The Grifters*, Roy realises that he is sexually attracted to his mother, but he again fails to understand that his mother's sexual advances to him are part of a thinly disguised plot to take his money, and he is subsequently (accidentally?) killed by her. In *House of Games*, Margaret recognises that she in fact is a 'born thief' and a 'booster' and embarks on a repression-free life after she 'forgives herself' for killing(?) Mike (Joe Mantegna). Finally, in *Confidence* and *The Sting*, Jake and Hooker make amends for their original mistake (and the death of their respective partners in crime) by 'punishing' the King and Lonnegan respectively, while they realise the importance of calculating all the moves of the game in advance (something that both Jake and Hooker failed to do when they swindled a 'connected' mark in the opening sequences of *Confidence* and *The Sting*).

The above account clearly proves the validity of Neale's argument, as it is obvious that the generic specificity of the con artist film relies on the different weight given to the elements which it shares with other genres, in particular with the crime film and its subcategories. It remains to be seen how the above discourses are inscribed 'across more specific generic elements' and how they are articulated within specific cinematic codes.[28] To address the first question, I shall focus on the systems or horizons of expectation that the con artist film invites the spectator to form, while for the second issue I shall examine questions of filmic narration. The two questions are very much interrelated and invite some important answers to the problem of the specificity of the con artist film.

In terms of the first question, one could argue that the con artist film is characterised by a rather stable and clearly defined set of expectations that the spectators bring with them, and which, as Neale has argued, 'interact with films themselves during the course of the viewing process'.[29] In this respect, the 'contract' between film spectators and con artist films is as strong as the contracts between film spectators and other, more traditional, film genres such as the western and the musical, where 'the spectator must process what is seen and heard [and the film] must permit the spectator to derive pleasure from its fictional play'.[30] Specifically, the contract drawn between con artist film and spectator specifies that the film offers a particular type of story which is likely to contain an unusually large number of narrative twists and surprises, which the spectator is invited to guess throughout the course of viewing from the opening sequence to the final credits. Spectators are invited, therefore, to bring along some finely tuned cognitive skills, which will help them navigate through the, often extremely dense, plots that con artist films are structured around. Given the con artist film's axiomatic dependence on plots structured around characters who steal, cheat, deceive, lie and betray, it comes as no surprise that the key task the spectator is asked to perform is to distinguish between lies and truth or fiction and reality (within the diegesis), which in most of the above films are articulated in an extremely complex fashion.

What becomes obvious, then, is that the main objective for the film spectator is to understand the film's narrative, a task which is required of the spectator from all film genres, though for many con artist films it is likely to require multiple viewings (something which is definitely the case for *The Spanish Prisoner*, as I suggested in the previous chapter). In this respect, what differentiates the con artist film as a genre from other film genres is that it actively challenges the spectator to comprehend the narrative, almost as a matter of principle. Unlike other film genres where narrative comprehension is invited as a matter of fact, the con artist film challenges the spectator's cognitive skills to understand the narrative to an extent that is rarely seen in other genres in US cinema. When a film 'stack[s] enough multiple deceptions and surprise turnabouts', or 'is a devilishly clever series of reversals that keeps you guessing to the very end', as *Variety* remarks about *Confidence* and *The Spanish Prisoner* respectively, the spectator's cognitive skills assume a considerably more important role in the process of narrative comprehension than in other genres. Consequently, spectators enter the viewing process with their cognitive skills on full alert in order to deal successfully with the con artist film's relentless attempt to 'beguile, surprise and disorient them'. These are characteristics which Leslie Kane specifically identified in Mamet's films, and which are constitutive characteristics of the con artist film as a genre and of *The Spanish Prisoner* as a characteristic example of this genre, and in particular of its subcategory, the con game film.

It is obvious, then, that the discourses of human nature in general and of human psychology in particular are strongly inscribed – via the emphasis on spectators' cognitive skills – across the set of expectations that comprise the con artist film. This strong link, however, gives way to a paradox that lies at the core of the con artist film. While, as noted earlier, the narrative of the con artist film depends on the failure of a character's cognitive ability to recognise the truth behind appearances, the spectators' pleasure depends on the reverse, namely on the successful application of their cognitive skills in recognising the truth behind appearances. Unlike the con artist film characters who do not know whether they are being conned or not at any given point in the narrative, the spectators expect that every single encounter between characters can potentially be a con (or part of a con under way), that every shot, sequence and scene can potentially be a clue which will help them put together the pieces of a (narrative) puzzle. Predicting the con, anticipating the twist, identifying the 'mark' in advance all become parts of the spectator's pleasure in a category of films where predictability is by definition under attack. This is especially so when 'the cumulative expectation and knowledge of the audience', which according to Richard Maltby and Ian Craven is 'central to the operation of any genre movie',[31] has created even more complicated con artist film narratives (two recent examples would be *Confidence* and *Criminal*). Here the spectator's pleasure takes the form of expecting the unfolding of the con in even more unpredictable ways. Central to this process, of course, is the function of filmic narration.

As the mechanism that controls 'the overall regulation and distribution of knowledge which determines *how* and when the spectator acquires knowledge, that is, how the spectator is able to know what he or she comes to know in a narrative',[32] narration is by definition of the utmost significance in con artist films. Despite Branigan's emphasis on 'how', questions of 'when' the spectator acquires knowledge are equally crucial, given the con artist film's indisputable propensity towards narrative twists which depend entirely on the narration's withholding of vital information until particular moments in the narrative. For that reason, it is not only the information that narration withholds from the spectator during the course of the narrative that takes primary position in the overall organisation of the con artist film's narrative structure, but also the time that narration takes to reveal this information to the spectator. It could, then, be argued that narration in con artist films works towards a particular arrangement of narrative information, which is geared towards timely revelations of previously undisclosed information. This arrangement primarily aims at surprising and, occasionally, shocking the spectator, through the creation of a number of narrative twists and reversals, unless the spectator reaches those points of revelation earlier. This function of narration is particularly evident in the subcategory of the con game film, but it is easily noted in all con artist films.

Not surprisingly, the game of creating narrative twists that the narration constantly arranges for the pleasure of the spectator in the con artist film brings together several of the discursive categories that are associated with the general discourse of human nature which is mobilised by the narratives of this type of films, as noted earlier. The narration's propensity towards challenging the spectators' cognitive skills in order to surprise them matches fully the con artists' panache in elaborate tricks which dupe unsuspecting (that is, non-alert) characters in the diegesis. Discursive categories such as perception, cognition and, more generally, the workings of the human mind are, therefore, masterfully imbricated across the code of filmic narration, all contributing to the generic specificity of the con artist film.

The Con Game Film

The narrative in con artist films like *Confidence* is usually structured around a swindler or, more often, a group of swindlers who apply the tricks of their trade to unsuspecting characters, with the main objective of acquiring material wealth. The placing of such characters in the position of a protagonist, whose psychological motivations and actions drive the narrative forward, however, constitutes an important aesthetic choice for the filmmakers working within the genre. By locating the swindler at the epicentre of action, con artist films actively seek the spectators' complicity in at least some aspects of the crime (planning, execution, erasing traces of the crime, etc.) he or she commits. In this respect, the spectators' alignment with the con artist/protagonist necessarily involves questions of complicity on their part, mainly because the spectators are allowed (always partial) knowledge of the con, which effectively makes them invisible gang members who hope that the con job will succeed. To this end, it is the job of the narration to keep the spectator in doubt about the outcome of the con(s) by withholding crucial information from the beginning, information that will be revealed in time during the course of the narrative. Besides the example of *Confidence* I noted above, this type of narrative structure and function of narration can be also found in films such as *The Sting*, *Traveller* and *The Grifters*.

Conversely, the narrative of a small number of films that includes Mamet's *House of Games* and *The Spanish Prisoner*, as well as *Matchstick Men* and, to a certain extent, *Criminal*, is structured around a protagonist who assumes the role of the victim in what turns out to be an elaborate con, rather than the perpetrator of it. In particular, the narratives of *House of Games* and *The Spanish Prisoner* are organised around the actions of Margaret and Joe, a psychiatrist and a corporate designer respectively, who fail to see that their encounters and transactions with a number of characters in the narrative are well-disguised, precisely calculated moves in con games designed to make them hand $80,000 and a 'process', respectively, to con artists. Equally, the narratives of *Matchstick Men* and *Criminal* revolve around the actions of two con artists, Roy and Richard, who, despite knowing the tricks of the trade, find themselves handing $300,000 and $60,000 respectively to fellow swindlers. I would like to argue that this is a distinct category within the con artist film genre and I will term this group of films the con game film, precisely because the emphasis lies on the trick, scheme or swindle, and in particular on the moment of recognition by protagonist and spectator alike. This means that all the narrative events were in actual fact building blocks in an elaborate con game that is not revealed as such until the very end of the films.

The similarities between this small group of con game films and the broader category of the con artist film I discussed above are obvious. The disruption of the narrative equilibrium and the restoration of order in the con game film follow the same pattern (emphasis on the failure of a character's cognitive skills in perceiving the truth, mobilisation of the key discourse of human nature, challenging the spectator to comprehend the narrative, and so on). The main difference between the two categories, however, lies in the role of the filmic narration, which in the con game film assumes a fundamentally different role from that it has in the con artist film.

Specifically, narration in the con game film works towards concealing any information that would lead the spectators to suspect that a con is taking place, suppressing almost all available clues that would help them order the narrative information correctly. This, therefore, challenges further the spectators' cognitive skills in their attempt at narrative comprehension. More importantly, by structuring the film narrative around the story of a character who ends up being the 'mark' of a con, narration in the con game film ensures that the spectators occupy a similar position to the protagonist; that is, the spectator also becomes a 'mark', the mark in the unfolding of a story. Having a false sense of security that they control the narrative through the psychologically motivated actions of a protagonist who also (falsely) believes that he or she is in control of all events and transactions, the spectators come in for a shock when they realise at the end of the film that neither the protagonist nor they 'had a clue' about the real nature of the narrative events (as is the case with the scene when 'the process' is switched over which I discussed in Chapter 4).

In order to achieve the above objective effectively, narration in con game films presents an unusual degree of restrictedness to the actions of the main character. In all the above four films, the protagonists are present in virtually every scene of the narrative, which allows the unfolding of the story to be filtered solely through their individual perspectives. These perspectives are always presented by the narration as reliable and steadfast, since in the initial stages of all four narratives each protagonist is represented as a 'knowledgeable' individual who is very good at what he or she does (Margaret's career as a psychiatrist is on the up, Joe has just discovered a formula that can predict global market changes, Roy is a very successful con man and Richard scores much bigger cons than Rodrigo). As a result, the spectator has no reason not to invest in the credibility of the protagonists as intelligent characters who are more likely to be the perpetrators of the cons the films are expected to unfold, rather than the actual marks.[33] For that reason, part of the surprise or shock the spectators experience at the end of those films is due to the investment they have made in the knowledgeableness of the protagonist.

One of the most important functions of the restricted (to the perspective of the mark) narration in the con game film is that it prevents the spectator from knowing that a con targeting the protagonist is under way. By denying the spectator access to narrative events outside the protagonist's sphere of knowledge, the narration is able to present narrative information mono-dimensionally, a characteristic which should alert at least the cine-literate spectator. It is at this point, however, that the protagonist's status as a knowledgeable and intelligent character becomes important, as exactly these traits work to reassure the spectator that the protagonist should be capable of intercepting any suspicious signals and exposing any scam under way.

The unusually restricted narration, however, has a second function: to surprise and shock the spectator in much more forceful ways than the narration in the con artist films. Given the fact that all information throughout the narrative of con game films is filtered through one perspective (which is falsely perceived as knowledgeable, intelligent and adequate), the revelation of the real nature of the narrative events can take on very surprising, even shocking dimensions, depending on the height of the stakes.

In the light of the challenge that restricted narration presents for the spectator's narrative comprehension of the con game film, they respond by employing two information-processing techniques, one of which assumes a more important role than the other. The spectator resorts to the pool of knowledge of the genre accumulated from their interaction with other con game films (top-down approach) or look for clues that the narration has not successfully managed to suppress or has even subtly planted (bottom-up approach). Although the top-down approach to the narrative is significant in preparing the spectator for the different directions the narrative can take (including the surprising revelation at the end), as well as in placing the spectator's bottom-up approach on solid foundations, it is the bottom-up approach itself that is mainly responsible for the spectator's pleasure in the con game film.

Despite the extreme extent of the narration's restrictedness, the spectator is always afforded certain clues and, if careful, he or she can obtain information not accessible to the central character. These clues can take several formats, such as rare omniscient moments, frames specifically composed to convey information only to the spectator, meanings conveyed by the juxtaposition of shots and, generally, other techniques associated with a film's *mise en scène*, cinematography, editing and sound. But in order for the spectator to be successful in this pursuit of superior knowledge (to the protagonist), he or she must question from the start the protagonist's perception and intelligence, as they are never as adequate as the narration would have them appear. Even in this case, however, the spectator has often to deal with a narration that can and does resort to unreliability at critical stages during the course of the narrative. At this point even the most alert of spectators has no alternative means at their disposal to anticipate the specifics of the outcome of the narrative trajectory. It is at this moment that the spectator realises that he or she was set up by the narration to occupy the position of the mark, just like the protagonist.

The Oldest Con in the Book: *The Spanish Prisoner* as a Con Game Film

In the introduction to this book I discussed how approximately 18 minutes into the film there are three scenes that involve Joe and Susan on a plane back from the Caribbean islands, which, even though they seem to be about Joe's efforts to swindle his way to Susan's attention, turn out, instead, to be building blocks of an extremely elaborate con of which Susan is a part and which is designed to make Joe hand over 'the process'. Joe's misconception about Susan's objective is founded on his belief that he is in control of the exchange between them, a belief that, as I argued earlier, is characteristic of a person not knowing his or her part or position in any situation. The spectator, however, despite being aligned from the beginning of the narrative with Joe, is in a position to anticipate the protagonist's misconception and thus disengage from his (limited) perspective, which the filmic narration privileges. It is at this point that the spectator's knowledge of the genre (through previous interaction with other texts), and his or her top-down approach to the narrative, can come in handy. The avid con artist/con game genre viewer should respond much more quickly and sceptically than the 'average Joe' to the numerous repetitions of axiomatic (for the genre) truths that Susan utters. In particular, the phrase 'that's what you just think you saw', which Susan utters in response to Joe's firm belief that he saw Jimmy Dell coming out of a plane (and not out of a boat that came from the direction of the plane), was also used in Mamet's other con game film, *House of Games*, in a scene where the con artists demonstrate to Margaret how a number of con tricks work. This should lead the viewer to adopt a much more cautious attitude to Susan, something that Joe cannot do. Having outlined the manner in which con games are played at the level of the scene and how the spectator might be implicated, I am moving on now to discuss narrative structure, narration and the role of the spectator at the level of the film.

The narrative begins with a business trip that a few employees of a company, including Joe Ross, the film's protagonist, take to the island of St Estephe in the Caribbean. After a fade in, the first shot reveals a sign in an airport that reads:

Did you pack your own bag?
Are you carrying gifts or packages for someone you don't know?
Has your bag been out of sight since you packed it?

Almost immediately after registering the information on the sign, the camera tilts down and tracks in towards a security X-ray monitor which shows a number of bags passing through it. After lingering for a few seconds on the monitor, the camera continues its tracking movement to reveal two men, Joe and George Lang, walking.

Even from the first shot, the spectator is given a number of clues about the nature of the narrative. The camera's emphasis on the airport sign and the X-ray screen foreshadows future narrative events (Joe's realisation that he is carrying a package for someone he does not know, his placing of a gun through an X-ray screen, etc.). However, and more significantly, it informs the spectators about crucial questions they need to keep in mind for the purposes of narrative comprehension. This first shot also introduces the key idea of the film, namely, that people one thinks one knows might not be what they appear to be. Essentially, then, the opening shot functions as a *mise en abyme* for the whole film as it 'designates the economy of mean(ings) with which a [Hollywood] opening prepares the stage and often presents the whole film in a nutshell'.[34]

Having introduced the main premise of the film in the first shot, the rest of the early scenes of the film (the scenes that take place in St Estephe) introduce the main characters and their state of affairs. Two very significant events take place during the unfolding of this part of the narrative. First, Mr Klein, Joe's boss, evades acknowledging Joe's role in the invention of 'the process' and equally evades settling the matter of his bonus for his work. Second, Joe meets a mysterious millionaire, who comes to the island with his mistress, and ends up spending the evening and the early hours of the following day in his company. The first event signifies the end of the equilibrium in the narrative. After Klein's refusal to reassure Joe about his bonus, a refusal which Joe construes as part of the company's strategy to avoid paying him for his work (but which in actual fact is the first kick-off in the con game), Joe starts feeling uneasy about his future, and all his further actions are permeated by that. On the other hand, his meeting and subsequent relationship with Jimmy Dell establish Joe's only contact besides his work colleagues, which, of course, becomes instrumental later in the narrative when Joe becomes increasingly convinced that his company is, indeed, trying to find ways around paying him for his work and he therefore cannot trust his colleagues.

However, the real nature of the above events (precisely calculated moves in a con game designed to make Joe hand 'the process' over to a crew of con artists) is not revealed to the spectator until very late in

Figure 6 Loud noise interrupts the discussion and signals Susan's change of subject

the narrative. At this early stage, the spectator has no reason either to suspect Klein's postponement of settling Joe's bonus as an attempt to avoid paying him or to doubt Jimmy Dell's status as a well-off man on a romantic trip with his mistress. In fact, the film's narration uses the first encounter between Dell and Joe as a proof of Dell's status. Assuming that a photograph Joe took of Susan features him and his mistress, Dell approaches Joe and offers him $1,000 for his camera. Dell's behaviour, which codes him as a rude man who thinks that money can buy everything, helps establish him in the mind of Joe and the spectator as a wealthy man who is very sensitive about his private affairs.

The spectator is none the less not kept entirely in the dark, despite the lack of any hard evidence about the unfolding of a con game, at this stage of the narrative. Having entered the viewing process with a fairly stable set of expectations about the film (anticipation of various directions that the narrative can take; an unusual number of twists; labyrinthine plots structured around people who steal, cheat and lie for a living; and so on), the spectator is constantly trying to guess what he or she is not told and shown by the narration. For this reason, despite not having a concrete reason to suspect that Klein or Dell might have different agendas in mind, the spectator can and certainly does 'expect the unexpected'. This is all the more so if he or she picks up a couple of subtle clues that the narration has planted for the spectator's benefit.

In these early scenes, these clues take the form of 'signals' that specific characters seem to be sending to other characters off screen. The first of these clues takes place in the scene on the beach when Joe and Susan (and the spectator) hear the loud noise of a plane flying very close to the beach (Figure 6). Prior to this point, Susan and Joe have been having a casual conversation about whether it would be appropriate for Susan to call Joe by his first name. Suddenly they both stop walking and talking for a moment as the overwhelming, off screen noise of a plane's engines draws their attention to it. As soon as the noise fades away and we get a shot of the plane on course to land (Figure 7), Susan starts asking questions about Joe's earlier meeting with the investors, insisting that she understands that it is something very big, a view that Joe does not do anything to dismiss. The loud noise of the plane can be perceived as a signal for Susan, to inform her that the part of the con when Dell appears

Figure 7 The plane with which Dell 'arrives' on the island

in the picture is about to take place and to start her questions about Joe's meeting. In this second conversation, Susan's objective is to come across as interested in Joe and also as fishing for some information, as she is in the lowest position in the company hierarchy and wants to know more (something that will be picked up again later in the narrative when Joe says that everybody needs to feel important). Additionally, Susan is to take a picture of Joe at the time when Dell appears in the background.

The second clue is provided in the scene where Dell apologises for offering money to Joe during their first meeting, and involves Dell's casual dropping of a tennis ball to the court. After expressing his apologies, Dell invites Joe for a drink. With a slight delay, Joe, who until that point has been spending the evening on his own, accepts the invitation and gets up from his seat. As the two men walk away from the camera, Dell casually throws behind him a tennis ball he has been holding throughout the duration of the scene. The camera lingers for a few seconds on the ball (Figures 8 and 9) before a dissolve moves the narrative a few hours later. Like the sound of the plane engines, the dropping of the tennis ball could be seen as a signal that informs the rest of the gang that everything is going according to plan.

Figure 8 Dell drops the ball

Figure 9 Another signal?

Although the above clues are so subtle that they can be easily missed even by the most alert of spectators, other pieces of information that the narration provides prove to be red herrings (of a different, much subtler kind than the excessive red herrings I discussed in the previous chapter). One particularly prominent piece of information that the narration presents several times throughout the narrative, the involvement of 'the Japanese' in the plot to steal 'the process', later proves to be the ultimate con that the film narration plays on the spectator. From the beginning of the film, 'the Japanese' are established as 'a group of people' who have a particular interest in 'the process'. In short, they are established as characters the spectator should watch closely in the unfolding of the narrative, expecting that at some point they will try to get their hands on 'the process'. This piece of information is provided for the first time in the second scene of the film when Joe singles out 'the Japanese' as the people most likely to have an interest in stealing 'the process', and thus personalises the neutral term 'competition' that all other participants in the meeting use. Following that scene, there are a number of shots where Japanese tourists are present, with their presence noted almost each time by the main characters: in St Estephe as honeymooners; in New York outside the car dealership; at the tennis club; at the Boston airport; on the shuttle bus; and on the boat to Boston. Despite their presence in the above shots, no Japanese character attempts to steal 'the process' until the penultimate scene of the film, when the narrative momentarily seems to be taking such a direction. However, the following and last scene of the film reveals that 'the Japanese' were not 'the competition', but rather, people working for the US Marshals Service.

This final twist was one of the few totally unexpected directions of the narrative trajectory, with no clues whatsoever offered by the film's narration about the presence of the law.[35] In fact, the final narrative surprise depends entirely on the absence of any such clues, especially in the penultimate scene when the 'Japanese' man withholds his identity from Joe. The withholding of this piece of information encourages the protagonist and the spectator to assume (wrongly) that the competition have, at long last, revealed themselves. This is so until the following scene, when protagonist and spectator alike once again discover that 'you don't know who anyone is'. In a very short span of time, therefore, the identity of one person changes from a Japanese tourist to a Japanese con artist to a US marshal.

The scenes on the island and on the plane back to New York, which constitute the set-up of the film, are indicative of the function of the narration in the con game film. Completely restricted to the protagonist's perspective and very uncommunicative, the narration withholds all concrete pieces of information that would lead the spectator to suspect that a con is under way. Occasionally, the narration becomes somewhat more communicative by offering a few subtle clues to the spectators, challenging them to predict the direction the narrative will take but, also, often sending them in the wrong direction through the disclosure of information that eventually proves wrong (the Japanese interest). As a result, the spectator has the difficult task of distinguishing between the real clues and the diversions, the times when the narration is reliable and the times when it lies, which of course mirrors the protagonist's task within the diegesis.

Ass well as in the final scene of the film, which was not preceded by any clues pointing in that direction, the difficulty of the spectator's task becomes even more evident in the scene where Joe signs his name on the membership form he is handed at the private club (Figure 10). The shot consists of a close-up of the membership form as Joe writes his signature, and lasts two seconds. Despite a club employee holding the form from the top edge, the alert spectator can discern the letters CLU BER IP

Figure 10 Joe is 'clearly' getting ready to sign a club membership decree

DECREE before the employee's hand covers the rest of the letters. At this point, the spectators assume that if they had seen the title of the form it would read CLUB MEMBERSHIP DECREE. The spectator who missed the above information would also believe that what Joe signed was a membership form for entry to the club. However, when the police later present the same form to Joe (Figure 11) and accuse him of planning to run away to Venezuela, a country with no extradition treaty with the United States, the title of the form reads CONSULADO DE VENEZUELA. This constitutes a shocking and totally unexpected development for the second type of spectator, the ones who did not notice the letters on the form in the earlier club scene. These spectators will at this point realise that they placed too much trust on the film's narration as well as on their 'indexical' understanding of what type of form Joe signed.

For the spectator who noticed the letters on the form in the club scene, however, this is a more shocking development, since it questions the spectators' actual senses and, in particular, their sight. But having no other alternative (unless they decide to view the film again), the alert spectator is led to believe that the title CLUB MEMBERSHIP

Figure 11 The form that Joe signed was an asylum request to the government of Venezuela

DECREE was 'what they thought they saw' and consequently accepts the narration's confidence game as reality. It is tricks like these that con game films perform, making famous film critic Roger Ebert proclaim *The Spanish Prisoner* as 'delightful in the way a great card manipulator is delightful. It rolls its sleeves above its elbows to show it has no hidden cards, and then produces them out of thin air.'[36]

The rest of the narrative is arranged according to similar narrational techniques, so it is not surprising that *The Spanish Prisoner* (as well as the other con game films) requires more than one viewing to ensure complete narrative comprehension, or to be more precise, to determine the film's narrative logic. The last-minute revelation that Joe's narrative agency had been completely undermined by an invisible gang of con artists from the beginning of the film, to the extent that all his (seemingly) psychologically motivated actions were in actual fact reactions to a game set up by others, demands at least one more viewing of the film. This is in order to determine narrative agency (to become aware of the parts every character plays in the con), and to look for further clues.

This problem of narrative agency in the con game film in general, and in *The Spanish Prisoner* in particular, raises the question of the extent to which con game film narratives can be seen as classical narratives from a different perspective, and reiterates the point I have made in the previous chapter about Mamet's uneasy relationship with contemporary (classical) Hollywood cinema.

Despite all the evidence that suggests that the film belongs to the con game genre, *The Spanish Prisoner* has been overwhelmingly received by critics as a thriller, while the presence of a clear McGuffin ('the process' everyone tries to steal) has led many critics to add the adjective 'Hitchcockian' before the above generic category.[37] Even Mamet himself was quick to attach this label to his film when he described it in an interview with Robert Denerstein:

Denerstein: *The Spanish Prisoner* . . . may remind you of the kind of thriller Hollywood turned out during the 1930s and 1940s. The resemblance is not accidental.

Mamet: To me *Spanish Prisoner* falls into the tradition of the light romantic thriller. The form of the light thriller, as far as I can tell, was created by Hitchcock. The form is quite straightforward. There's the guy on the run. There's the girl who helps him. There are powerful people whose friends turn out to be the bad guys. There's the denouement in an extraordinarily improbable place. There's the deus ex machina, in which help comes from a place where there's no possible help, and everything made right in the last twenty seconds.[38]

The above, rather broad, account of *The Spanish Prisoner*'s generic status as a (light romantic) thriller does not do the film justice. First, some of the above formal characteristics exist only in a piecemeal fashion and are expressed very late in the film. For instance, Joe goes on the run only in the last third of the narrative after discovering that he has been framed for George Lang's murder, while Susan's 'help' does not materialise until a few scenes later, approximately twenty-five minutes from the film's end. The delay in the manifestation of those formal characteristics clearly problematises the film's status as 'the innocent-on-the-run thriller', a subcategory of the suspense thriller that Charles Derry has identified,[39] and which Mamet seems to allude to.

Additionally, and if one saw beyond the above problem, Derry's definition of 'the innocent-on-the-run thriller', as a film that is 'organised around an innocent victim's coincidental entry into the midst of global intrigue',[40] might fit like a glove for films like Hitchcock's *North by Northwest* (1959), *The Man Who Knew Too Much* (1955) and *The 39 Steps* (1939), all of which were compared to Mamet's film. However, it is totally inapplicable to a film where coincidences are only a matter of appearance and the innocent victim's entry into a not so global world of corruption is not coincidental but the product of a well-designed plan.[41] Furthermore, and even more problematically, the above account is so broad that it can be easily applied to films belonging to other genres. For example, what stops a western or a science fiction film from demonstrating exactly the same characteristics that Mamet invests the thriller with? A film such as *The Matrix* (Andy and Larry Wachowski, 1999) can also be seen to revolve around a man on the run (Thomas A. Anderson/Neo); a woman who helps him (Trinity); powerful people whose friends turn out to be bad guys (the agents); a denouement that occurs in an improbable (literally and metaphorically speaking) place (at the ship when Neo dies); a *deus ex machina* who offers help when there is literally no hope (Trinity and her confession of love for the hero); and a happy ending in the last seconds of the film (Neo exterminates the agents and starts destroying the Matrix). This suggests that there are other, 'more specific generic elements' that must be examined by the critic, elements which point towards the existence of an alternative generic framework within which Mamet's film can be located. This framework is that of the con game film.

Conclusion

Irrespective of the reluctance of the critical apparatus to accept the existence of the con artist and the con game film as generic frameworks with a distinct identity, and of the filmmaker's and critics' persistence in attaching the 'light romantic thriller' label to *The Spanish Prisoner*, as this chapter has demonstrated, the con artist and con game film do exist as genres and Mamet's film is a particularly good example of the latter. In this respect, alongside the views of critics of the film who saw it as a 'playful exercise in twisting plausibility and expectations', an 'exercise in teasing and tantalising' and a 'continuation of his [Mamet's] search for an answer to Joe Mantegna's enquiry in *House of Games*: What's more fun than human nature?',[42] one should also add that *The Spanish Prisoner* is an exercise in filmmaking within the rules and conventions of the con game film.

Conclusion

The Spanish Prisoner is a characteristic example of American 'indie' cinema, irrespective of the fact it has not been perceived as such by either popular or scholarly film criticism. The film's truly unique but, at the same time, stagy aesthetic, in tandem with the filmmaker's stubborn decision to put the mechanics of the plot before verisimilitude and/or psychological motivation, and the presence of a strong genre framework (which, arguably, is more appropriate for mainstream Hollywood cinema) made for a 'curious' type of film that, not surprisingly, puzzled film critics. It seems that the film's relatively humble industrial origins and the filmmaker's distinct aesthetic stamp were firmly at odds with the crowd-pleasing subject matter and the concrete conventions of the con game genre within which it operated. After all, despite the success of several genre films like *From Dusk Till Dawn*, and despite the production of more upmarket films by Miramax and the third wave of the classics divisions, the 'indie' sector was still perceived to be about films with offbeat subject matter and gritty visual style, neither of which characterised Mamet's film.

One could go as far as to argue that both subject matter and style in *The Spanish Prisoner* were 'wrong' for an 'indie' film. In terms of the former, the mechanics of the elaborate con trick that takes place on several locations (including an exotic island in the Caribbean) are hardly the material of the esoteric or offbeat stories that characterised other key 'indie' films in 1997–8, such as *The Opposite of Sex, Henry Fool, In the Company of Men, Buffalo '66* (Gallo, 1998) and *Happiness* (Solondz, 1998). Equally, in terms of style, Mamet's admittedly distinctive visual style was a far cry from the visceral, camerawork-based, 'cinematic' *tour de force* that came to characterise celebrated 'indie' films released around the same time as *The Spanish Prisoner*, such as *Boogie Nights, Pi* or *Jackie Brown*. In this respect, *The Spanish Prisoner* was not only a film that did not fit with mainstream Hollywood; it was also a film that did not fit with American 'indie' cinema, which explains why critics ignored the film's 'indie' roots (and Sony Pictures Classics' marketing efforts) and saw the film as yet another output from the remarkably prolific – in a variety of media – David Mamet. It was Mamet who, in the critics' view, functioned as the preferred overarching reception framework for the film at the expense of the reception framework represented by 'indie' cinema.

If *The Spanish Prisoner* did not fit with American 'indie' cinema, however, this was with an increasingly amalgamated, crystallised and institutionalised American 'indie' cinema, which, as Schamus would triumphantly proclaim a year after the film's release, 'had won its battles'.[1] By the mid-1990s, this institutionalised 'indie' cinema had looked increasingly for more commercial fare, for films that would not alienate the large mainstream audience (irrespective of how idiosyncratic they might be in terms of aesthetics or subject matter), for films that had the potential to transcend their budget limitations by becoming crossover box-office hits (and pay for the box-office failure of similar films that did not manage to find an audience). It was this institutionalised 'indie' cinema that had started achieving considerable public visibility, and *The Spanish Prisoner* with its several commercial points seems to fit the description well.

However, this was only on paper. In reality, Mamet's film was a throwback to the times before the institutionalisation of that type of cinema, to the times when experimentation, stylisation and idiosyncrasies could assume any form and take any direction, irrespective of whether the final product would alienate potential larger audiences or would consciously damage the film's success at the box office. It would not be widely off the mark to speculate that *The Spanish Prisoner* could have been a respectable box-office success if it had been made as a mainstream film, without Mamet's 'entomologically exact, detached direction',[2] and 'without the studied blankness of his house acting style [that] keeps you at one too many removes from his characters'.[3] After all many of the films he has written that have been directed by other filmmakers have become great box-office successes.

However, this is beside the point. For the purposes of this book, what is important is that Mamet utilised the resources of this institutionalised American 'indie' cinema to continue making hugely distinctive films that refuse to succumb to aesthetic trends, whether these trends are oppositional to mainstream cinema or not. In this respect, he has remained true to the objective of independent cinema; that is, to offer a real commercial alternative to Hollywood entertainment. In the process he has been able to carve a remarkable (and unique) filmmaking career at the margins of Hollywood, in spite of the box-office failure of most of the films he has written and directed. And *The Spanish Prisoner* represents the epitome of Mamet's filmmaking: unsettling, uncompromising, individualistic. For all those reasons it stands as a true example of American 'indie' cinema.

Filmography: David Mamet in American Cinema and Television

As Writer/Director

House of Games (1987, Orion, US, 102 min.)
Things Change (1988, Columbia, US, 100 min.)
Homicide (1991, Triumph Releasing Corporation, US, 102 min.)
Oleanna (1994, Samuel Goldwyn Company, US, 89 min.)
The Spanish Prisoner (1997, Sony Pictures Classics, US, 110 min.)
The Winslow Boy (1998, Sony Pictures Classics, US, 104 min.)
State and Main (2000, Fine Line Features, US, 105 min.)
Heist (2001, Warner, US, 109 min.)
Spartan (2004, Warner, US, 106 min.)
Redbelt (2008, Sony Pictures Classics, US, 99 min.)

As Screenwriter

The Postman Always Rings Twice (Rafelson, 1981, MGM/Lorimar, US, 122 min.)[1]
The Verdict (Lumet, 1982, Fox, US, 129 min.)[2]
The Untouchables (De Palma, 1987, Paramount, US, 119 min.)[3]
We're No Angels (N. Jordan, 1989, Paramount, US, 101 min.)[4]
Hoffa (De Vito, 1992, Fox, US, 140 min.)
Vanya on 42nd Street (Malle, 1994, Sony Classics, US, 119 min.)[5]
The Edge (Tamahori, 1997, Fox, US, 117 min.)
Wag the Dog (Levinson, 1997, New Line Cinema, US, 97 min.)[6]
Ronin (Frankenheimer, 1998, MGM/UA, US, 121 min.)[7]
Hannibal (R. Scott, 2001, Universal, US, 131 min.; co-written with Steven Zaillian)[8]

As Screenwriter Adapting his Own Plays for the Cinema

Glengarry Glen Ross (Foley, 1992, New Line Cinema, US, 100 min.)
American Buffalo (Corrente, 1996, Samuel Goldwyn Company, US, 88 min.)
Lakeboat (Mantegna, 2000, Cowboy Bookings International, US, 98 min.)
Edmond (Gordon, 2005, First Independent, US, 82 min.)

As Screenwriter Adapting his Own Plays for Television

A Life in the Theater (K. Browning and G. Gutierrez, 1979, PBS, US)
The Water Engine (Schachter, 1992, Amblin/Brandman/Majestic Films, US, 110 min.)
A Life in the Theater (Mosher, 1993, US, 78 min.)

As Screenwriter for Television Films

Uncle Vanya (Mosher, 1991, WNET Channel 13, US)[9]
Texan (T. Williams, 1994, Directed By, US, 26 min.)
Lansky (McNaughton, 1999, HBO, US, 112 min.)[10]

As Creator/Writer/Director for Television

The Unit (2006–)[11]

As Director for Television

Catastrophe (2000, BBC/Film Four, GB, 6 min.)[12]
The Shield (2004, Fox Television Network, US)[13]

As Writer for Television Shows

Hill Street Blues (1981, NBC, US)[14]

Mamet's Plays Adapted for the Screen and Directed by Others

About Last Night . . . (Zwick, 1986, Columbia TriStar, US, 113 min.)[15]

Notes

Introduction

1 Earlier scenes clearly established that senior staff in the company do not socialise with the secretaries. For instance, in the scene in the beach bar we see Klein and the potential investors at one table, Joe and Lang at another and Susan sitting at the bar socialising with an FBI agent. Furthermore, George Lang in particular seems to have a genuine aversion to the possibility of socialising with a secretary. At one point he asks Joe whether it was his imagination or the secretary did indeed travel first class with them.

2 Anon., 1999, p. 65.

3 Hamilton, 1998, p. 40.

4 McNab, 1998, p. 14.

5 For instance, Ruth Barton labels the film 'a thriller' which 'visually and thematically . . . belongs to the current neo-noir cycle' (1998, p. 40); Alexander Walker calls the film a 'puzzle' (1998, p. 27); while Geoffrey McNab calls the film 'a hugely enjoyable thriller.'

6 McNab, 1998, p. 14.

7 For comparisons with *The 39 Steps* and *North by Northwest* see McNab (1998, p. 14); Greenberg (1998, p. 88), Taubin (1998, p. 68) and Rosenbaum (1998, p. 152). For comparisons with *The Usual Suspects* see Kemp (1998, p. 53) and Taubin (1998, p. 68).

8 Tzioumakis, 2008, pp. 154–5.

9 Tzioumakis, 2006a, p. 247.

Chapter 1

1 Quoted in Turner, 1997.

2 All the box-office figures for *Independence Day*, *Twister* and *Mission Impossible*

were taken from BoxOffice Guru: http://www.boxofficeguru.com (last accessed 28 June 2008).

3 Turner, 1997.
4 Rosen and Hamilton, 1990, p. 186.
5 Levy, 1999, p. 279.
6 Biskind, 2005, p. 234.
7 McCarthy, 1997.
8 This self-definition of the Sundance Channel was taken from the channel's website: http://www.sundancechannel.com/about/FAQ (last accessed 28 June 2008).
9 Again this self-definition was taken from the service's website: http://www.indiewire.com/about (last accessed 28 June 2008).
10 The box-office figures for *Fargo, Sling Blade* and *From Dusk Till Dawn* were taken from the Internet Movie Database: http://www.imdb.com (last accessed 28 June 2008).
11 Biskind, 2005, p. 81.
12 The box-office figures for all those films were taken from the Internet Movie Database: http://www.imdb.com (last accessed 28 June 2008).
13 Although Columbia/TriStar is cited here as one entity (as TriStar was a subsidiary of Columbia Pictures), in later tables TriStar will be classed as a major distributor in its own right, therefore making the number of major Hollywood distributors eight (and not seven).
14 King, 2005, p. 37.
15 Dawes, 2003, p. 12.
16 Biskind, 2005, p. 11.
17 Vachon was quoted in Biskind, 2005, p. 165.
18 Tzioumakis, 2006a, p. 247.
19 Medavoy, 2004.
20 The figures were taken from the release dates provided at the Internet Movie Database (http://www.imdb.com, last accessed 28 June 2008). The release dates are for the official release of a film in the US and do not include early releases as part of festival screenings. In this respect, *The Spanish Prisoner* appears as a 1998 release even though it was first screened in the Toronto International Film Festival in 1997.
21 These figures were taken from the Internet Movie Database (last accessed 28 June 2008).
22 Anon., 1996, p. 13.
23 Wyatt, 1998, pp. 86–7.
24 Wyatt, 1998, p. 84.

25 Biskind, 2005, p. 139.
26 The figure was taken from the Internet Movie Database (last accessed 28 June 2008).
27 See http://www.fox.co.uk/searchlight/ (last accessed 28 June 2008).
28 O'Rorke, 2003, p. S1.
29 Tzioumakis, 2006a, p. 265.
30 Brodesser, 2003, p. 55.
31 The box-office figure was taken from the Internet Movie Database (last accessed 28 June 2008).
32 McNary, 2004, p. 5.
33 See the company's website http://www.unitedartists.com/ (last accessed 28 June 2008) and Carver, 1999.
34 Quoted in O'Rorke, 2003, p. S-1.
35 Quoted in Media Rights, available online at http://www.mediarights.org/about/our_partners.php (last accessed 28 June 2008).
36 Schamus, 2002, p. 253.
37 Schamus, 2002, p. 254.
38 The figures were taken from Box Office Guru (last accessed 28 June 2008).
39 King, 2005, p. 9.

Chapter 2

1 Exceptions here are Tzioumakis (2006a, pp. 240–3) and Tzioumakis (2008), which examine Mamet's *House of Games* as an independent film. Tzioumakis has also examined the filmmaker as an example of an industrial auteur associated with independent cinema (2006b, pp. 60–75). The current chapter is a revised version of that particular essay.
2 See Brewer (1993) and Burton (2005).
3 Jones, 2007, p. 8.
4 Levy, 1999, p. 2.
5 Mamet, 1990, p. 119.
6 James, 1998, p. 24.
7 For instance, John Harrop and Sabin R. Epstein have classified Mamet's work within a postrealist tradition (which in their book is equated with the theatre of the absurd; 2000, p. 221). On the other hand, Michael Quinn has located Mamet's work within a realist tradition, albeit one where mimesis has given way to performed actions, an expressive rather than representational realism (1996, p. 235).

8 On the history of Orion Pictures see Tzioumakis (2004, pp. 87–135).

9 Brown, 1992, p. 29.

10 McGilligan, 1980, p. 31.

11 Tzioumakis, 2006a, p. 231.

12 For positive reviews of *House of Games* see in particular Lesser (1988, p. 27) and Ebert (1999). The box-office figure was taken from the Internet Movie Database, available at http://us.imdb.com/title/tt0093223/business (last accessed 30 June 2008). Unless otherwise stated all the box-office figures in this chapter were obtained from the Internet Movie Database and were last accessed 30 June 2008.

13 For a warm review of *Things Change* see Ebert (1988); for a negative review see Kauffman (1988, pp. 26–7).

14 Between 1988 and 1991 Mamet's only involvement in American cinema was the script for Paramount's *We're No Angels*.

15 Although *We're No Angels* proved a modest box-office failure, *The Postman Always Rings Twice* and *The Verdict* were both great financial success (with the latter grossing $54 million), and *The Untouchables* was one of the highest-grossing films of 1987, scoring $77 million at the US box office.

16 Equally, Mamet did not receive any concrete credit for his script for *Hoffa*. Interestingly, Fox advertised the feature as 'A Danny De Vito film', thus focusing on the celebrity status of the actor-director (despite the fact that the phrase 'a Danny De Vito film' does not signify any distinct thematic or stylistic characteristics).

17 Significantly, *The Edge* was produced by Art Linson and starred Alec Baldwin (both close friends and regular collaborators in Mamet's films). Still, there have been rumours that Mamet worked on various scripts for the majors but without credit or under pseudonym. Perhaps the most persistent such rumour is that he worked on the script for John Frankenheimer's *Ronin* (1998) under the name Richard Weiss.

18 The US box-office takings for *Heist* were a little under $25 million. This figure was obtained from Box Office Guru at http://www.boxoffice-guru.com/h.htm (last accessed 30 June 2008).

19 See for instance the trailer for Miramax's *Kill Bill Vol. 1*, which advertises 'the fourth movie', refusing for some time to supply any more information. It is obvious that Miramax addresses Tarantino fans who are aware of his filmography, to the extent that neither his name nor his previous three films have to be mentioned.

20 Mamet, 1994, p. 107.

Chapter 3

1 Bennett Pozil of Natexis Bank Populaire was quoted in Seguin, 2001, p. 13.
2 Merritt, 2000, p. 411; King, 2005, p. 36.
3 Turan, 1998.
4 Roman, 1998.
5 Fleming, 1993.
6 Mamet, 1998c.
7 Rudolph, 1998, pp. 40–8.
8 Mamet has always adhered to the axiom 'all mistakes are made in pre-production' and therefore has made meticulous preparations for all his shoots (Mamet, 1990, p. 125).
9 Rudolph, 1998, p. 42.
10 Kelly and Hindes, 1997.
11 Hindes, 1998b.
12 Kelly, 1997.
13 Kelly and Hindes, 1997.
14 The information about the film's participation in festivals was taken from the film's profile in *Variety*, available online at http://www.variety.com/profiles/Film/main/30941/The+Spanish+Prisoner.html?dataSet=1 (last accessed 26 June 2008).
15 Klain, 1983b.
16 Clark, 2006.
17 Bart, 2005.
18 Grove, 2001.
19 Klain, 1983a.
20 Thompson, 2006.
21 Rooney, 2004, p. 8.
22 Harris, 2003, p. 54.
23 Mohr, 2005, p. 1.
24 See Tzioumakis, 2004, pp. 100 and 109.
25 The box-office figure was taken from the Internet Movie Database, online at http://www.imdb.com/title/tt0104454/business (last accessed 26 June 2008).
26 Anon., 1995.
27 Hernandez, 2002.
28 By evoking Maslin and Turan by name, it is clear that the trailer targets the arthouse audiences in New York and Los Angeles, who often use

these two critics' reviews in their decision-making when it comes to film-going.

29 The full poster, complete with reviews, taglines and credits, can be found in the Internet Movie Poster Awards, available at http://www. impawards.com/1998/spanish_prisoner.html.

30 Hunter, 1998.

31 Unless otherwise stated, all the box-office figures in this chapter were taken from *The Numbers*, 'a resource for industry professionals and fans to track business information on movies.' The site contains a detailed chart about the film's box-office performance, online at http://www.the-numbers.com/movies/1998/0SPRS.php (last accessed 26 June 2008).

32 According to industry definitions a limited release normally involves films that at no point are screened in more than 600 cinemas.

33 According to a *Variety* article, even by its eighth week the film continued posting over $10,000 average per screen in Los Angeles and New York. See Hart and Roman (1998).

34 Klady, 1998.

35 Hindes, 1998a.

36 Roman, 1999.

Chapter 4

1 Kaufman, 1998.

2 Trifonova, 2002, p. 23.

3 Trifonova, 2002, p. 23.

4 Thompson, 1999, p. 10.

5 Thompson, 1999, pp. 12–13.

6 Allen and Gomery, 1985, p. 81.

7 Tzioumakis, 2008, pp. 168–9.

8 Shone, 1998.

9 Kemp, 1998.

10 Greenberg, 1998.

11 Turan, 1998.

12 Gilbey, 1998.

13 Bolton, 1998.

14 For a comprehensive discussion of practical aesthetics see Mamet, 1998a; and Bruder et al., 1986.

15 Mamet, 1998b, p. 37.

16 Mamet, 1990, p. 120.

17 In his writings on film, Mamet has added the word 'stupid' after the 'keep it simple' axiom as a form of homage to the collective power of the audience to read in advance the trajectory of a scene. Hence, 'Keep It Simple, Stupid' (1990, p. 124).

18 Mamet, 1998b, p. 73.

19 It's worth noting here that Mamet's use of Eisenstein's theory of montage is on a basic level (the combination of two shots corresponds to a concept) and therefore does not involve any political purposes or meanings that the work of the Soviet filmmaker and theorist did.

20 Mamet, 1998b, p. 66.

21 Mamet, 1998b, p. 30.

22 In discussing the quest of the hero Mamet directly refers to Hitchcock and the McGuffin, something that a number of reviews highlighted in relation to *The Spanish Prisoner*. As Mamet put it, the hero's goal need not be concrete but may be 'a loose abstraction' which 'allows audience members to project their own desires on an essentially featureless goal' (1998b, p. 29).

23 Mamet, 1998b, p. 30; original italics.

24 Mamet, 1992, p. 3.

25 Like the 'blocking of the scene', the terms 'through line' and 'through action' stem from Stanislavsky's theories of acting.

26 Mamet, 1994, pp. 202–3.

27 Williams, 1998.

28 Denby, 1998.

29 I am indebted to Eleftheria Thanouli for suggesting this point.

30 Bordwell, 1997, p. 33.

31 Barton, 1998, p. 41.

32 Rosenbaum, 1998, p. 153.

33 In the opening of the film, Joe writes on a blackboard how much money his invention is projected to bring to potential investors, but the figure is written off screen, so the spectator stands to see only the investors' reaction.

34 The conversation was transcribed from the DVD version of the film, Region 2, distributed by Pathé, 1999.

35 Mamet, 1990, p. 64.

36 Mamet, 1994, p. 202 – original italics.

37 In this respect, this stylistic choice is different in nature from a choice such as the break of the 180-degree rule I discussed earlier, which, of course is only perceptible to the spectator.

38 Taubin, 1998, p. 68.
39 Bolton, 1998.
40 See, for instance, Queenan (2001, pp. 12–13); Romney (1999, pp. 2–3); and DePino (1998, pp. 7 and 11).
41 Turan, 1998.
42 Mamet, 1994, p. 203 – original italics.
43 See Tzioumakis, 2006c, pp. 88–99.
44 Maltby and Craven, 1995, p. 247.
45 As Maltby and Craven have put it: 'Acting manuals [in Hollywood cinema] invoke an idea of 'truth' in performance almost as often they invoke the rhetoric of realism' (1995, p. 247).
46 Curtis, 1998, p. 22
47 Barton, 1998, p. 41.

Chapter 5

1 Arthur Magida of the *Baltimore Jewish Exponent*, quoted in Kane, 1999, p. 263.
2 Kane, 1999, p. 262.
3 Leitch quoted in Kane, 1999, p. 263.
4 Kane, 1999, p. 263.
5 Ryall quoted in Neale, 2000, p. 12.
6 The first quotation is from Fisher (1998, p. 27). The second is from Sweet (1998, p. 5).
7 Neale, 2000, pp. 71–85.
8 For instance, Maitland McDonagh labels *The Grifters* as a 'film noir' (1990, p. 30); Tim Applegate uses the terms 'thriller' and 'film noir' to discuss the same film (1999); B. Ruby Rich refers to *The Grifters* as 'neo-noir' (1995, p. 8); as does Steve Neale, who also attaches the same label to *House of Games* (2000, p. 175); 'neo-noir' is also the label attached to *The Spanish Prisoner* by Ruth Barton (1998, p. 40); Anton Bitel uses five different terms ('crime', 'drama', 'thriller', 'film noir' and 'heist film') to determine the generic context of *Confidence* (2003); Paul West calls *Matchstick Men* a 'caper film' (2003), and finally, Emanuel Levy has approached *Traveller* as a 'comedy-adventure' (1997) while *USA Today* critic Mike Clark called the film a 'comedy-drama' (1997).
9 Lukow and Ricci quoted in Neale, 2000, p. 39.
10 Patterson, 1990, p. xv.
11 Patterson, 1990, p. xvi.

12 *Oxford English Dictionary Online*, 2nd edn, online at http://dictionary.oed. com.ezproxy.liv.ac.uk/cgi/entry/50046042? (last accessed 2 July 2008).

13 *Oxford English Dictionary Online*, 2nd edn, online at http://dictionary.oed. com.ezproxy.liv.ac.uk/cgi/entry/50046042?/ (last accessed 2 July 2008).

14 The quotation was referenced as taken from the novel's 1951 edition, p. 310. *Oxford English Dictionary Online*, 2nd edn, online at http://diction- ary.oed.com.ezproxy.liv.ac.uk/cgi/entry/50046042? (last accessed 2 July 2008).

15 The reference of the film's publicity to more than one genre categories supports Rick Altman's observation that advertising during the studio times almost always evoked 'not a single genre but multiple genres' (Altman, 1998, p. 7). However, Altman's discussion, which covers films such as *Only Angels Have Wings*, *Dr Ehrlich's Magic Bullet* and *The Story of Alexander Graham Bell*, does not extend to determining whether the evoked genres are placed in a hierarchical structure with one dominat- ing the others.

16 The extracts from all the reviews (with the exception of those for *The Grifters* and *House of Games*) were taken from *Variety Online*. Specifically, for *Confidence* see Rooney (2003); for *Matchstick Men* see McCarthy (2003); for *The Spanish Prisoner* see Klady (1997); for *Traveller* see Levy (1997); for *The Sting* see Variety Staff (1972). The review for *The Grifters* was taken from *Variety* (1991) and that for *House of Games* was taken from *Variety* (1989).

17 These subdivisions of the thriller and the suspense thriller were intro- duced by Charles Derry and have been cited in Neale, 2000, pp. 82–3.

18 Special features: 'Anatomy of a Scene' in *Confidence*, DVD, Region 1, US, Lions Gate Films, 23 min.

19 Special features: 'Production Notes' in *Traveller*, DVD, Region 1, US, October Films.

20 Kay, 2003, p. 27.

21 Consider for instance an example from *Bend It Like Beckham* (Chadha, 2002). In one sequence Jesminder, the protagonist, 'convinces' her mother to give her money to buy shoes for her sister's wedding. On receipt of the money, our heroine uses some of this money to buy the shoes for the wedding, but she uses a substantial sum to buy football boots, despite her mother's explicit order to stop playing football. Even though one could certainly argue that Jesminder conned her mother so that she can buy professional football boots, her act would never be considered a crime in the legal meaning of the term.

22 Neale, 1980, pp. 22–3
23 Neale, 1980, p. 20.
24 Neale, 1980, pp. 20–1.
25 Neale, 1980, p. 21.
26 All quotations in this paragraph are from Neale, 1980, p. 21.
27 Nadel, 1997, p. 124.
28 Neale, 1980, p. 21.
29 Neale, 2000, p. 31.
30 Krutnik, 1991, p. 5.
31 Maltby and Craven, 1995, p. 124.
32 Branigan, 1992, p. 76 – original italics.
33 This is especially true in the case of *Matchstick Men* and *Criminal*, two films whose protagonists are con artists by profession but who come to occupy the position of the mark of a con by the end of the film.
34 Elsaesser and Buckland, 2002, p. 47.
35 An exception here is the presence of a police detective who questions Joe when 'the process' is (seemingly) stolen from him, and who explains to him in the end that Klein was the person behind the organisation of the con.
36 Ebert, 1998.
37 See for instance Rosenbaum, 1998, p. 152; Gilbey, 1998.
38 Denerstein, 2001, p. 227.
39 Derry in Neale, 2000, p. 83.
40 Derry in Neale, 2000, p. 83.
41 This is also the case with the other films I have included in the con game film category: *House of Games*, *Matchstick Men* and *Criminal*.
42 Gilbey, 1998; McNab, 1998; Anon., 1999.

Conclusion

1 Schamus, 2002, p. 253.
2 Andrew, 1998, p. n/a.
3 Shone, 1998.

Filmography

1 Adapted from James M. Cain's novel *The Postman Always Rings Twice* (1934).
2 Adapted from Barry Reed's novel *The Verdict* (1980).

3 Adapted from Elliot Ness, Paul Robsky and Oscar Fraley's novel *The Untouchables* (1957). The film is also loosely based on the television series *The Untouchables* (1959–63, ABC) which was adapted from the 1957 novel as well.

4 The film is a loose remake of *We're No Angels* (Curtiz, 1955, Paramount, 106 min.), which was based on Samuel and Bella Spewack's play *My Three Angels* (1953). The play was an English adaptation of Albert Husson's French play *La Cuisine de Anges*. Although Mamet's screenplay has retained a few elements of the original story (the escaped convicts from Devil's Island, their attempt to escape the authorities, the fact that the convicts are good-hearted), the narrative of the 1989 film nevertheless does not bear any resemblance to the story of the 1955 film.

5 Mamet co-wrote the screenplay with André Gregory. Anton Chekhov also has a screenwriter's credit, as the film is about a group of New York actors rehearsing *Uncle Vanya*.

6 The screenplay was co-written by Mamet and Hilary Henkin and is based on Larry Beinhart's novel *American Hero* (1993).

7 Mamet co-wrote the screenplay with J. D. Zeik under the pseudonym Richard Weiss. The screenplay is based on a story by Zeik.

8 Mamet wrote the screenplay for *Hannibal*, which was based on Thomas Harris's novel *Hannibal* (2000). Steven Zaillian is credited as co-author of the film's screenplay, even though it was his version of the script that was used for the film.

9 Vlada Chernomordik is credited with the literal translation of Chekhov's play, whilst Mamet is credited as the film's screenwriter.

10 Mamet wrote the screenplay based on Dennis Eisenberg, Uri Dan and Eli Landau's novel *Mayer Lansky: Mogul of the Mob* (1979).

11 Mamet created this prime-time television show in 2006 and at the time of writing it is in its fourth season. The show is based on Eric L. Haney's book of the same title. Haney was a founding member of Delta Force, arguably the best-known anti-terrorist unit in the USA. Mamet has writing credits as creator in all episodes (59 at the time of writing) and has directed four: 1.06, 'Security'; 1.13, 'The Wall'; 2.06, '*Old Home Week*'; and 4.01, 'Sacrifice'.

12 *Catastrophe* (1984) is a short play by Samuel Beckett. In 2000, 'Beckett on Film', a project financed by RTÉ and Channel 4, invited nineteen filmmakers (including Neil Jordan, Atom Egoyan, Karel Reisz, David Mamet and Anthony Minghella) each to adapt one of Beckett's plays for

the screen. Mamet adapted and directed *Catastrophe*, which features John Gielgud's last film performance.

13 Mamet directed episode 3.11, entitled 'Strays' (broadcast on US TV on 4 May 2004). The episode features Mamet's wife and regular actress in his films, Rebecca Pidgeon.

14 Mamet scripted this early episode of the successful television series *Hill Street Blues* (1981–7), entitled 'A Wasted Weekend'.

15 The screenplay was by Tim Kazurinsky and Denise DeClue and is very loosely based on Mamet's *Sexual Perversity in Chicago*.

Bibliography

Allen, Robert C. and Douglas Gomery (1985) *Film History: Theory and Practice*, McGraw-Hill, London.

Altman, Rick (1998) 'Reusable Packaging: Generic Products and the Recycling Process' in Browne, Nick (ed.) *Refiguring American Film Genres: Theory and History*, University of California Press, Berkeley, pp. 1–41.

Andrew, Geoff (1998) '*The Spanish Prisoner*' in *Time Out*, 28 Aug., p. n/a.

Anon. (1995) 'The Big Question: Can It Find Boxoffice Magic Again?' in *Hollywood Reporter*, 1 Aug., p. 13.

Anon. (1996) 'Sony Pictures Classics' in *Hollywood Reporter*, 1 Aug., p. 13.

Anon. (1999) 'DVD review of *The Spanish Prisoner*' in *Sight and Sound*, Vol. 9, No. 4, p. 65.

Applegate, Tim [1999] '*The Grifters*' in *Kamera*, online at http://www.kamera.co.uk/features/the_grifters.php (last accessed 20 June 2008).

Bart, Peter (2005) 'Sony Classics' Class Act' in *Variety*, 23 May, p. 4.

Barton, Ruth (1998) '*The Spanish Prisoner*' in *Film Ireland*, No. 67, Oct./Nov., pp. 40–1.

Biskind, Peter (2005) *Down and Dirty Pictures: Miramax, Sundance and the Rise of Independent Film*, Simon and Schuster, London.

Bitel, Anton [2003] '*Confidence*' in *Movie Gazette*, online at http://www.movie-gazette.com/cinereviews/393 (last accessed 20 June 2008).

Bolton, Chris A. (1998) '*The Spanish Prisoner*' in *24 Frames per Second*, online at www.24framespersecond.com/reactions/films_s/spanishprisonerbolt.html (last accessed 7 Dec. 2000).

Bordwell, David (1997) *On The History of Film Style*, Harvard University Press, Cambridge, MA.

Branigan, Edward (1992) *Narrative Comprehension and Film*, Routledge, London.

Brewer, Gay (1993) *David Mamet and Film: Illusion/Disillusion in a Wounded Land*, McFarland, Jefferson.

Brodesser, Claude (2003) 'Fox: A Brighter Searchlight' in *Variety*, 7 April, p. 55.

Brown, Clarence (1992) 'Down the Drain with the Ninja Turtles: Hollywood's Last Creative Sanctuary Has Fallen to the Vultures' in *The Guardian*, 6 Feb., p. 29.

Bruder, Melissa, Lee Michael Cohn, Madeleine Olnek, Nathaniel Pollack, Robert Previto, and Scott Zigler (1986) *A Practical Handbook for the Actor*, Vintage Books, New York.

Burton, Bruce (2005) *Imagination in Transition: Mamet's Move to Film*, Peter Lang, Bern.

Carver, Benedict (1999) 'UA Films to Make "Things": Garcia Helming Ensemble Cast' in *Variety*, 10 Aug., online at http://www.variety.com/article/VR1117750215.html (last accessed 28 June 2008).

Clark, John (2006) 'To Promote Unusual Films, Try Uncommon Marketing' in *New York Times*, 16 Jan., p. C5.

Clark, Mike (1997) '*Traveller*' in *Rotten Tomatoes*, online at http://uk.rottentomatoes.com/m/traveller/?page=2&critic=columns&sortby=date&name_order=asc&view=#mo (last accessed 20 June 2008).

Curtis, Quentin (1998) '*The Spanish Prisoner*' in *Daily Telegraph*, 28 Aug., p. 22.

Dawes, Amy (2003) 'DVDs Lead the Way for Recovery of Indie Film' in *Variety*, 17 Feb., Supplement, p. 12.

Denby, David (1998) 'Speaking in Tongues' in *New York*, 13 Apr., p. 48.

Denerstein, Robert (2001) 'Games Mamet Plays' in Kane, Leslie (ed.) *David Mamet in Conversation*, University of Michigan Press, Ann Arbor, pp. 226–39.

DePino, Dave (1998) '*The Spanish Prisoner*' in *Park La Brea News*, 30 Apr., pp. 7 and 11.

Ebert, Roger (1988) '*Things Change*' in *Chicago SunTimes*, 21 Oct., online at http://rogerebert.suntimes.com/apps/pbcs.dll/article?AID=/19881021/REVIEWS/810210305/1023 (last accessed 30 June 2008).

Ebert, Roger (1998) '*The Spanish Prisoner*' in *Chicago SunTimes*, 24 Apr., online at http://rogerebert.suntimes.com/apps/pbcs.dll/article?AID=/19980424/REVIEWS/804240303/1023 (last accessed 20 June 2008).

Ebert, Roger (1999) '*House of Games*' in *Chicago SunTimes*, 31 Oct., online at http://rogerebert.suntimes.com/apps/pbcs.dll/article?AID=/19991031/REVIEWS08/910310301/1023 (last accessed 30 June 2008).

Elsaesser, Thomas and Warren Buckland (2002) *Studying Contemporary American Film: A Guide to Movie Analysis*, Arnold, London.

Fisher, Nick (1998) 'Scam-tastic' in *The Sun*, 29 Aug., p. 27.

Fleming, Michael (1993) 'Woody Exits Tristar for Sweetland Deal' in *Variety*, 21 July, online at http://www.variety.com/article/VR108904 (last accessed 25 June 2008).

Gilbey, Ryan (1998) '*The Spanish Prisoner*' in *The Independent*, 27 Aug., p. 13.

Greenberg, James (1998) 'Identity Crisis' in *Los Angeles Magazine*, Apr., p. 88.

Grove, Christopher (2001) 'Crouching Indie' in *Variety*, 14 May 2001, p. 35.

Hamilton, Jake (1998) '*The Spanish Prisoner*' in *Empire*, Sep., p. 40.

Harris, Dana (2003) 'H'wood Renews Niche Pitch: Studios Add Fresh Spin as They Rev Up "Art" Divisions' in *Variety*, 7 Apr., pp. 1 and 54.

Harrop, John and Sabin R. Epstein (2000) *Acting with Style*, Allyn and Bacon, London and Boston.

Hart, Amelia and Monica Roman (1998) '"Prisoner" Again Tops Exclusives' in *Variety*, 27 May, online at www.variety.com/article/VR1117471239.html (last accessed 26 June 2008).

Hernandez, Eugene (2002) 'Decade: Michael Barker & Tom Bernard – Another Ten Years in the Classics World. Part 2' in *Indiewire*, online at http://www.indiewire.com/people/int_DECADE_SonyClass_2A651.html (last accessed 26 June 2008).

Hindes, Andrew (1998a) 'Pike Joins as Partner in Shoreline Restructuring: Mamet-Helmed "Lakeboat" 1st Pic Under New Regime' in *Variety*, 9 Oct., online at http://www.variety.com/article/VR1117481275 (last accessed 26 June 2008).

Hindes, Andrew (1998b) 'Toronto Beckons "Basil": Pic Was Pulled from Last Year's Fest' in *Variety*, 13 July, online at http://www.variety.com/article/VR1117478392 (last accessed 26 June 2008).

Hunter, David (1998) '*The Spanish Prisoner*' in *The Hollywood Reporter*, 6 Apr., pp. 8–9.

James, Nick (1998) 'Suspicion' in *Sight and Sound*, Vol. 8, No. 10, Oct., pp. 22–4.

Jones, Kent (2007) 'On Your Mark' in *House of Games Booklet*, The Criterion Collection DVD, Special Features, pp. 1–11.

Kauffman, Stanley (1988) 'David Mamet: The Writer Fails the Director' in *New Republic*, Vol. 199, No. 19, pp. 26–7.

Kaufman, Gerald (1998) '*The Spanish Prisoner*' in *New Statesman*, 4 Sep., pp. 39–40.

Kane, Leslie (1999) *Weasels and Wisemen: Ethics and Ethnicity in the Work of David Mamet*, Macmillan, London.

Kay, Jeremy (2003) 'Close Up: James Foley' in *Screen International*, No. 1396, 14 Mar., p. 27.

Kelly, Brendan (1997) 'Sad, "Sweet" Toronto Bows' in *Variety*, 5 Sep., online at http://www.variety.com/article/VR1116675215 (last accessed 26 June 2008).

Kelly, Brendan and Andrew Hindes (1997) 'Arthouse Labels Busy at Toronto' in *Variety*, 12 Sep., online at http://www.variety.com/article/VR1116674805 (last accessed 26 June 2008).

Kemp, Philip (1998) '*The Spanish Prisoner*' in *Sight and Sound*, Vol. 8, No. 9, Sep., p. 53.

King, Geoff (2005) *American Independent Cinema*, I. B. Tauris, London.

Klady, Leonard (1997) '*The Spanish Prisoner*' in *Variety*, 21 Sep., online at http://www.variety.com/review/VE1117329519 (last accessed 20 June 2008).

Klady, Leonard (1998) 'Summer Burns Up B.O. Records: "Mary", "Truman" Surprise Studios' in *Variety*, 8 Sep., online at http://www.variety.com/article/VR1117480173 (last accessed 26 June 2008).

Klain, Steven (1983a) 'Orion Adds a "Classic" Accent: Bernard, Gigliotti Set New Unit' in *Variety*, 8 Apr., pp. 3 and 31.

Klain, Stephen (1983b) 'Prods Over-Value US Art Mart: Classics Eye Upfront Stakes as Terms Stiffen' in *Variety*, 4 May, p. 532.

Krutnik, Frank (1991) *In a Lonely Street: Film Noir, Genre, Masculinity*, Routledge, London.

Lesser, Wendy (1988) 'Mamet Unmasked' in *The Threepenny Review*, Spring, p. 27.

Levy, Emanuel (1997) '*Traveller*' in *Variety*, 23 Mar., online at http://www.variety.com/review/VE1117341893.html (last accessed 20 June 2008).

Levy, Emanuel (1999*)* *Cinema of Outsiders: The Rise of American Independent Film*, New York University Press, New York and London.

McCarthy, Todd (1992) '*Glengarry Glen Ross*' in *Variety*, 31 Aug., online at http://www.variety.com/review/VE1117901738 (last accessed 20 June 2008).

McCarthy Todd (1997) 'Final Cut at Sundance: Winter Fest Slates 103 Pix' in *Variety*, 4 Dec., online at www.variety.com/article/VR1116678801.html (last accessed 28 June 2008).

McCarthy, Todd (2003) '*Matchstick Men*' in *Variety*, 2 Sep., online at http://www.variety.com/review/VE1117921674 (last accessed 20 June 2008).

McDonagh, Maitland (1990) 'Straight to Hell' in *Film Comment*, Vol. 26, No. 6, Nov.–Dec., pp. 30–1.

McGilligan, Patrick (1980) 'Breaking Away Mogul Style' in *American Film*, Vol. 5, No. 8, June, pp. 28–32.

McNab, Geoffrey (1998) 'Why Less Is More' in *The Independent*, Review Section, 21 Aug., p. 14.

McNary, Dave (2004) 'Par Reinventing Classics' in *Variety*, 4 Oct., p. 5.

Maltby, Richard and Ian Craven (1995) *Hollywood Cinema: An Introduction*, Blackwell, Oxford.

Mamet, David (1990) *Some Freaks*, Faber and Faber, London.

Mamet, David (1992) *On Directing Film*, Faber and Faber, London.

Mamet, David (1994) *A Whore's Profession*, Faber and Faber, London.

Mamet, David (1998a) *True and False: Heresy and Common Sense for the Actor*, Faber and Faber, London.

Mamet, David (1998b) *3 Uses of the Knife: On the Nature and Purpose of Drama*, Columbia University Press, New York.

Mamet, David (1998c) 'Director's Interview' in *The Spanish Prisoner: A Sony Pictures Classics Release*, online at www.sonypictures.com/classics/spanishprisoner/main.html (last accessed 26 June 2008).

Maslin, Janet (1998) 'From Mamet. A Con Game. Secrets. Very Complicated' in *New York Times*, 3 Apr., online at http://query.nytimes.com/gst/fullpage.html?res=9C0DE7D8173AF930A35757C0A96E958260 (last accessed 20 June 2008).

Medavoy, Mike (2004) interview with the author, 15 June 2004, Los Angeles, California, 1 hour.

Merritt, Greg (2000) *Celluloid Mavericks: A History of American Independent Film*, Thunder's Mouth Press, New York.

Mohr, Ian (2005) 'Too Big for Their Niches: Specialty Arms Are Angst-Ridden as Studios Shake Up Biz Plans' in *Variety*, 21 Mar., pp. 1–41.

Nadel, Alan (1997) *Flatlining on the Field of Dreams: Cultural Narratives in President Reagan's America*, Rutgers University Press, New Brunswick.

Neale, Stephen (1980) *Genre*, BFI, London.

Neale, Steve (2000) *Genre and Hollywood*, Routledge, London.

O'Rorke, Michael (2003) 'Indies Inc.: In Today's Indie Landscape, Studio Specialty Divisions Seem To Have All the Advantages. But Is that Really Such A Bad Thing?' in *Hollywood Reporter*, 20 Mar. 2003, p. S1.

Patterson, Stephen (1990) 'Introduction' in Patterson, Stephen (ed.) *Herman Melville's The Confidence Man: His Masquerade*, Penguin, London, pp. vii–xxxvi.

Queenan, Joe (2001) 'Hick Flick' in *The Guardian*, The Guide, 10 Feb., pp. 12–13.

Quinn, Michael L. (1996) 'Anti-Theatricality and American Ideology: Mamet's Performative Realism' in Demastes, William (ed.) *Realism and the American Dramatic Tradition*, University of Alabama Press, Tuscaloosa and London, pp. 235–54.

Rich, B. Ruby (1995) 'The Neo Noir' in *Sight and Sound*, Vol. 5, No. 11, Nov., pp. 6–10.

Roman, Monica (1998) 'Miramax Gains "Celebrity": Allen Returns to Scene of Previous Triumphs' in *Variety*, 27 Apr., online at http://www.variety.com/article/VR1117470156 (last accessed 25 June 2008).

Roman, Monica (1999) 'Studio Report Card: Sony Pictures Classics: Diverse Slate Delivers Dinero' in *Variety*, 8 Jan., online at http://www.variety.com/article/VR1117489995.html (last accessed 26 June 2008).

Romney, Jonathan (1999) 'The Winslow Man' in *The Guardian*, Section B, 27 Aug., pp. 2–3.

Rooney, David (2003) *'Confidence'* in *Variety*, 27 Apr., online at http://www.variety.com/review/VE1117919732.html (last accessed 20 June 2008).

Rooney, David (2004) 'Niche Biz Comes into Focus: U Specialty Label Marries Taste with Overseas Savvy' in *Variety*, 2 Aug., pp. 8 and 15.

Rosen, David and Peter Hamilton (1990) *'Return of the Secaucus Seven'* in *Off Hollywood: The Making and Marketing of Independent Films*, Grove Weidenfeld, New York, pp. 179–95.

Rosenbaum, Jonathan (1998) 'Mamet and Hitchcock: The Men Who Knew Too Much' in *Scenario*, Vol. 4, No. 1, pp. 152–3 and 179.

Rudolph, Eric (1998) 'Paging Machiavelli' in *American Cinematographer*, Vol. 79, No. 3, Mar., pp. 40–8.

Schamus, James (2002) 'A Rant' in Lewis, John (ed.) *The End of Cinema As We Know It: American Film in the Nineties*, Pluto Press, London, pp. 253–60.

Seguin, Denis (2001) 'Round Table; Future of Film Financing' in *Screen International*, No. 1302, 30 Mar, p. 13.

Shone, Tom (1998) *'The Spanish Prisoner'* in *The Sunday Times*, Section II, 30 Aug., p. 4.

The Spanish Prisoner Profile in *Variety*, online at http://www.variety.com/profiles/Film/main/30941/The+Spanish+Prisoner.html?dataSet=1 (last accessed 26 June 2008).

Sweet, Matthew (1998) *'The Spanish Prisoner'* in *The Independent on Sunday*, 30 Aug., p. 5.

Taubin, Amy (1998) *'The Spanish Prisoner'* in *The Village Voice*, 4 Sep., p. 68.

Thompson, Anne (2006) 'Moving Pictures' in *Hollywood Reporter*, 17 Oct., p. n/a.

Thompson, Kristin (1999) *Storytelling in the New Hollywood: Understanding Classical Narrative Technique*, Harvard University Press, Cambridge, MA.

Trifonova, Temenuga (2002) 'Time and Point of View in Contemporary Cinema' in *Cineaction!*, No. 58, June, pp. 11–31.

Turan, Kenneth (1998) 'Life's a Charade in Mamet's *The Spanish Prisoner* Puzzle' in *Los Angeles Times*, 3 Apr., online at http://www.calendarlive.com/movies/reviews/cl-movie980402-5,0,4892028.story (last accessed 30 June 2008).

Turner, Dan (1997) 'For a Change Independent Films Get Both Acclaim and Good Box Office' in *Los Angeles Business Journal*, Vol. 19, No. 5, 3 Feb., online at http://findarticles.com/p/articles/mi_m5072/is_n5_v19/ai_19243321 (last accessed 28 June 2008).

Tzioumakis, Yannis (2004) 'Major Status – Independent Spirit: The History of Orion Pictures (1978–1992)' in *The New Review of Film and Television Studies*, Vol. 2, No. 1, May, pp. 87–135.

Tzioumakis, Yannis (2006a) *American Independent Cinema: An Introduction*, Edinburgh University Press, Edinburgh, p. 247.

Tzioumakis, Yannis (2006b) 'Marketing David Mamet: Institutionally Assigned Film Authorship and Contemporary American Cinema' in *The Velvet Light Trap*, No. 57, Spring, pp. 60–75.

Tzioumakis, Yannis (2006c) 'The Poetics of Performance in the Cinema of David Mamet: Against Embellishment' in *The Journal of the Midwest Modern Language Association*, Vol. 39, No. 1, Spring, pp. 88–99.

Tzioumakis, Yannis (2008) 'Entertainment in the Margins: Orion Pictures Presents a Filmhaus Production of a David Mamet Film' in Sickels, Robert C. (ed.) *The Business of Entertainment. Vol. 1: Movies*, Westview Press, New Haven, pp. 153–77.

Variety (1989) '*House of Games*' in *The Variety Reviews*, Vol. 20, 1987–1988, R. R. Bowker Publishing.

Variety (1991) '*The Grifters*' in *The Variety Reviews*, Vol. 21, 1989–1990, R. R. Bowker Publishing.

Variety Staff (1972) '*The Sting*' in *Variety*, 12 Dec., online at http://www.variety.com/review/VE1117488070.html (last accessed 20 June 2008).

Walker, Alexander (1998) 'Hooked by the Deceivers' in *The Evening Standard*, 27 Aug., p. 27.

West, Paul (2003) 'Cage's Character Is So Convincing in *Matchstick Men*' in *The Seattle Post Intelligencer*, 12 Sep., online at http://seattlepi.nwsource.com/movies/139167_matchstick12q.html (last accessed 20 June 2008).

Williams, Gaby (1998) '*The Spanish Prisoner*' in *The Guardian*, Section II, 28 Aug., p. 9.

Wyatt, Justin (1998) 'The Formation of the "Major-Independent": Miramax, New Line and the New Hollywood' in Neale, Steve and Murray Smith (eds) *Contemporary Hollywood Cinema*, Routledge, London, pp. 74–90.

Index